THUNDER ON
Bays Mountain

DALE E. GILBERT

NEWMAN SPRINGS PUBLISHING
320 Broad Street
Red Bank, NJ 07701

First originally published by Newman Springs Publishing 2021

Green Berry Gilbert and any person mentioned
as a member of his family are real.

Except for historical figures and events, all other characters
in this biographical novel are fictitious; and any resemblance
to living persons, present or past, is coincidental.

Last names of fictional characters may be
common to the East Tennessee area.

ISBN 978-1-63692-325-3 (Paperback)
ISBN 978-1-63692-326-0 (Hardcover)
ISBN 978-1-63692-327-7 (Digital)

Printed in the United States of America

To my wife, Peg, the love of my life, and Doug and Stacy, the most wonderful children in the world

The voice of the Lord is over the waters;
the God of glory thunders,
the Lord thunders over the mighty waters.

—Psalm 29:3 NIV

God's voice thunders in marvelous ways; He does
great things beyond our understanding.

—Job 37:5 NIV

How beautiful on the mountains are the feet of those who
bring good news, who proclaim peace, who bring good tidings,
who proclaim salvation, who say to Zion, Your God reigns!

—Isaiah 52:7 NIV

Contents

Foreword

The surname *Gilbert* means "pledge bright." It first gained popularity prior to and during the Norman conquest of Europe. The formation of the surname coincides with the Norman invasion of England in AD 1066 by King William I, usually known as William the Conqueror. He was born in Falaise, France, and was the first Norman king of England, reigning from AD 1066 until his death on September 9, 1087. His wife's name was Matilda.

Gilbert joined the family of popular Norman names because two of King William's close relatives bore the name of Gilbert. The Gilbert coat of arms consisted of a lion brandishing a battle-ax atop a castle turret.

Family roots have been traced back to the first known John Gilbert who was born in Madron, England, in 1640. Madron is a small village located in West Cornwall in South West England.

Several powerful Norman barons were Gilberts. During the Middle Ages, there were approximately 1,800 Englishmen named Gilbert. The Gilbert surname was chiefly located in the midland counties of England.

By the first census of America in 1790, many Gilberts had been recorded as settling in the new American colonies. The story as related in this book is told by Green Berry Gilbert, whose grandfather, John Gilbert "Bennett," was the first in our direct family to have immigrated here from England. A further explanation of the *Bennett* name will follow.

Getting to Know Me

My name is Green Berry Gilbert, the grandson of John Gilbert "Bennett." Most folks in this neck of the woods call me Green, GB, or Reverend. This "neck of the woods" is eastern Tennessee, specifically the area around Church Hill, located just a few miles west of Kingsport.

My life is not notable for any particular reason other than my great-great-grandson, the author of this book, thinks the picture of me and my beloved wife, Amanda, is so iconic in nature that there was probably a story to tell. The picture was taken around 1900 just outside the church I established on Bays Mountain in accordance with a land conveyance dated September 29, 1877.

The Bible I am holding has a covering made of squirrel skin and is opened to Hebrews 1:1–2. These are two of my favorite passages and are at the core of the Dunkard faith. We accept the Word of the New Testament as a revelation from heaven. This is the Bible I received from my older brother, John, right before he enlisted in the Confederate Army in June 1862. It had been given to him by our father, Harvey Greenville Gilbert. John said he did not want anything to happen to it while he was in the war, and that is why he gave it to me. I carried it throughout my service in the Civil War thinking that nothing would protect me more than carrying the Word of God.

The original Dunkard Church, shown here with members of our congregation, was located alongside the Bowser Cemetery on top of Bays Mountain, a short distance from Laurel Run. I was the minister of this church from 1878 until 1901 when I had to relinquish my duties due to poor health. This photo was taken around 1900 as well. Amanda is seated in the first row, seventh person from the left. Isn't she beautiful? The absolute love of my life!

One other picture I'd like to share is our home where we were blessed with nine children, eight of whom lived into adulthood.

That's me on the left coming out of the washhouse in my night shirt. Amanda is in the front yard with three of our daughters. The boys are not pictured and were probably squirrel hunting that day. And I can't forget our family dog, Walter, pictured in the foreground.

The home was located just a short distance from the church, and even though somewhat small, it was tidy and cozy. Amanda always did her best to make sure we were as comfortable as possible. Not an easy task with so many people under one roof.

Although you would never know it from our photo, we were young once and very much in love, as we were until the end. Everyone has a story to tell, and this is our story.

1775–1832

About the year 1775, at the age of fourteen, my grandfather, John Gilbert "Bennett," for reasons unknown, ran away from his home in the rolling hills and uplands of Derbyshire, England. Derbyshire is a county in the East Midlands area of England. Making his way to London, he found passage aboard the ship *Carolina* which set sail for Virginia.

Even though he was a young man at the time, there was some legend in our family history that my grandfather had a somewhat nefarious background in England prior to his immigration. That is the reason why he added the name *Bennett* to his name in a probable effort to throw the authorities off his trail. Once in America, he dropped the Bennett name.

Grandpa John was known as a kind and loving man, but his past was shrouded in mystery. The family never knew for sure why he fled England. My father, Harvey Greenville Gilbert, always said that Grandpa John kept a low public profile and seldom talked about his early youth in England. He had apparently fled England rather quickly.

Because these were Revolutionary War times in America, Grandpa had a fear that he would be sent back to England. Having a thick English accent, he was afraid he would be taken for a Loyalist to King George and immediately shipped back to the Mother Country. With this thought in mind, he quietly and eventually made his way to outstate Virginia, specifically Patrick County, where he hoped to "get lost" in America's young frontier.

He apparently succeeded in being somewhat anonymous. In December 1791, he purchased 144 acres of land on Spoon Creek in

Patrick County, for which he paid 30 pounds. Spoon Creek is about 167 miles southwest of Monticello.

Having settled into a quiet life of farming, he was united in marriage to Hannah Bussard in 1795; and to this union, my father, Harvey Greenville Gilbert, was born in 1811. Growing up in the Spoon Creek area of Patrick County, my father was exposed to all elements of an agricultural society. Unless you were a small-shop owner in one of the local towns, everyone else was involved in farming to make a living and feed their families. My father grew up in the rolling hills and valleys of the Piedmont Region and the Blue Ridge Mountains of Southwest Virginia. It was, and is, a beautiful part of Virginia.

My father grew up strong and resourceful; and at the age of twenty, he met and married the love of his life, Nancy Fee. They were married on Valentine's Day, February 14, 1831. In addition to a life of farming, my parents set about raising seven children before packing up and leaving for Hawkins County, Tennessee.

Grandpa John, having carved out a good life in America for his family, passed away in 1832.

1839–1859

I was born on July 23, 1839, in Patrick County, Virginia, the fifth of seven children born to Harvey Greenville and Nancy Fee Gilbert. My early life was shaped by hard work as we struggled to survive as a family.

Neither of my parents were formally educated, but they were smart enough to know that some general schooling just might give us an "edge" in life. My siblings and I attended a little one-room schoolhouse set in a bend on Spoon Creek. It was later enlarged to a two-room school which I attended until the eighth grade. By that time, I had a good basic learning of reading, writing, and arithmetic; and so I left school to work all day on the farm where my father said I was needed more. Even though my formal education was over, I continued to self-educate myself by reading everything I could get my hands on. A special reading time was late in the evening in front of the fireplace.

There was plenty of work to do for anyone of any size so long as you could lift or haul something. Planting, weeding, and feeding the animals was a constant job. Our growing family was up before dawn, ate a hearty breakfast, and by then had enough light to start working in the fields or garden. We had a few cows to milk, and the animals were fed before sunrise. Early on in my life, when I was less than ten, my father cut a hoe handle in half so that the hoe was short enough for me to use. You had to be creative to get the job done. Everybody worked! Mom and Dad called this our "avoiding-the-poorhouse program."

The 1840s and 1850s saw a great westward expansion of our country. In 1856, my father moved us from Patrick County, Virginia, to Bays Mountain, Hawkins County, Tennessee, near what is now Church Hill, a magnificently beautiful part of eastern Tennessee.

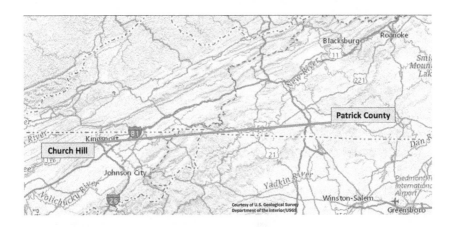

We moved because we had tried to eke out a living on the small parcel of land that Grandpa John had purchased, but by this time, many members of the family were trying to farm the same land—too many mouths to feed and not enough food to go around.

The distance from Spoon Creek, Virginia, to Bays Mountain, Tennessee, is approximately 189 miles, most of it through narrow dirt roads and mountain trails. We had two mules, Jingles and Buck, that pulled our wagon and a milk cow, Bootsie. We tied her to the wagon, which allowed her to trail along behind us. Most of our farm animals had names. Jingles was named because her harness had little bells that jingled when she walked. Buck was named because his hair was lightly brown, almost tan like a buckskin. Bootsie was a black-and-white cow, mostly black, and got her name from the white hair that partially ran up her legs from her hooves. The white hair made it look like she had on a pair of boots.

On July 7, 1857, just a few weeks before my eighteenth birthday, my father purchased seventy acres of land on the south side of Bays Mountain from John Crawford for the sum of $125.

Green Berry Gilbert

17

This is the first recorded presence of my family in the great state of Tennessee. Meshack Barrett had originally bought the property on April 7, 1826. It was then surveyed on April 18, 1827, by the county surveyor and subsequently sold to John Crawford and then to my father.

Bays Mountain is a section of the Ridge-and-Valley Appalachians, located in eastern Tennessee. It runs southwest to northeast, from just south of Knoxville to Kingsport, and is neatly tucked between the Blue Ridge Mountains to the southeast and the Appalachian Plateau to the northwest. Bays Mountain is just south of the Holston River, which flows from northeast to southwest.

Father always said the reason we moved to Tennessee from Virginia was so that we could create new and better lives for ourselves, our immediate families, and our heirs by taking advantage of the more fertile farmland. The first settlers had occupied the broad eastern valleys of the Tennessee and Holston Rivers. Like them, we thought this was a great place to begin a new life.

Our initial task after acquiring the property on top of Bays Mountain was to construct a simple small dwelling that could house five people: my mother, father, me, and younger siblings, Frances and Elisabeth. Older sisters, Lucinda, Sarah, and Hannah, plus older brother, John, had already married and left home. Log cabins were the mainstay as the typical East Tennessee farmhouse.

The next big projects were clearing the land and breaking the soil to plant several fields to put in food crops and a large garden for our vegetables. East Tennessee farming was characterized by smaller-scale subsistence farming. We planned to grow small-scale crops such as tobacco, wheat, and corn. Initially, though, we survived on goods we had moved with us from Virginia, plus wild fruits and game and garden vegetables that grew quickly until the first crop came in. We always had a large garden capable of growing sweet corn, turnips, green beans, peas, cabbage, tomatoes, onions, carrots, cucumbers, and squash. All of this took a great deal of tending to; and then when it was mature enough to harvest, we began the process of canning the fruits and vegetables for later use, primarily during the winter months.

Like nearly every neighbor around Bays Mountain and the Holston River area, my family planted corn as our main food crop. Corn was a perfect crop, and it did well in our newly cleared fields. We didn't have to tend to it much during the growing season; it produced many bushels on our small fields and gave us a main fixing for many other foods, such as bread and cornmeal.

We were also able to clear away enough timber to plant wheat since we were able to easily scatter it over the field. Our team of mules, Jingles and Buck, were very useful in breaking the ground with a plow and then cultivating it as well. Once the wheat was ready to be harvested, we used cradles, tiers, and shockers to bind the wheat into shocks so it could dry.

The timber that we cut to clear the fields was used to construct other outbuildings such as a smokehouse, tobacco barn, stock barn, and corn crib.

I've already mentioned our milk cow, Bootsie, but we also had a few hogs and chickens. These we bought or traded for from our neighbors or local livestock traders. The hogs we were able to acquire reproduced quickly, and they were pretty much able to take care of themselves. They were able to forage over most of our wooded land, but we had to make sure to keep them out of our fields and garden. This involved building strong fences to keep them out of the fields and garden and outbuildings to keep them in at night because of the wild animals that roamed the woods. One of the last things we did in the evening before going to bed was to fasten up the hogs. Pork became a staple meat for us since it was easy to preserve through curing and smoking. For these reasons, pork was the preferred meat among my family.

I learned a lot from taking care of our farm animals in my early years. As time went on, we were able to increase our livestock to a small herd and greatly increase the amount of chickens. The crops and vegetables we harvested from our fields and garden were now added to our beef, pork, and dairy products, such as butter and cheese.

There were many ways to prepare, cook, and preserve a variety of meats. Since pork was our preferred meat, we took great care to have large amounts on hand for our use. We especially liked to cook a hog or two in the summertime. The following processes worked extremely well for our large family and give a glimpse into how we lived. We didn't need recipe cards for these activities. It was just knowledge handed down from generation to generation.

We would slaughter a hog, and then

- cut it into pieces;
- unjoin the parts by cutting hams and shoulders in two or more pieces;
- likewise, the head and other parts;
- don't wait for the meat to cool;
- put the whole thing into a pot;
- use an outdoor ten-gallon kettle and then add enough water to start it cooking;
- continue cooking until thoroughly done and the water is cooked out of it;
- use plenty of salt and pepper for seasoning.

Set anywhere in a cool place, keeping it covered so that flies, dirt, cats, or dogs can't get to it. Believe me, we had plenty of all those things!

All of this was very convenient because at mealtime, we just took out of the kettle what we needed and then recovered it. The key is to always keep it covered. The meat kept sweet until we ate it all.

In July or August, when bacon gets strong, we are out of other meat, or just want a change, a pig weighing from fifty to one hundred pounds was killed and cooked in the same way. This process will keep meat lasting for two months or more.

To cure ham,

- rub the flesh side of the hams with plenty of cayenne pepper and the skin side with saltpeter;
- make a strong brine, enough to cover the hams;
- add to this brine, for every hundred pounds of meat, five ounces of saltpeter and two quarts of molasses;

- remain in pickle for four weeks;
- take them out of the pickle, wash the salt off, and cover with a coating of wheat bran;
- hang up the hams with the small end down and smoke with hickory or corncobs;
- when sufficiently smoked, wrap in paper, put into cotton packs, and hang in a dry, dark, cool place. Put away in the smokehouse before the flies come in the spring.

We put forth a great amount of effort in the preparation of food. It was, in reality, the difference between life and death. The processes were time consuming, but everyone pitched in and did their part.

Pork can also be pickled so that it will keep longer and stay fresher if necessary.

To pickle pork,

- the pork should lie twenty-four hours after being killed so that the animal heat can pass off;
- for the side meat, take one and a half pounds of brown sugar and one pint of salt for every fifty pounds of meat;
- rub the pieces well with it;
- sprinkle a thin layer of salt on the bottom of a clean sweet cask. A sweet cask is one in which the brine has never soured;
- place a layer of meat and another layer of salt and continue alternating until the meat is all in with a layer of salt on top;
- cover with a board and a weight to keep it under the brine.

To cure bacon,

- proceed the same as described above for pickled pork;
- when the meat has been in pickle three weeks, take from the brine, rinse, and wipe dry;
- hang up and smoke the same as hams.

To prepare meat before smoking,

- take one quart of sorghum molasses, one-half pound black pepper, and enough flour to make a thick paste;
- spread all over the meat that is not covered by skin;
- hang the meat up in the smokehouse;
- leave hanging as flies or bugs will not bother it;
- make sure the door to the smokehouse is latched or the cats might be a problem.

There is one more way to make meat last almost indefinitely, and that is to can it. We did a lot of this, and it sustained us over many cold winter months.

To can meat,

- take some nice scraps of meat, whether it's beef, pork, chicken, rabbits, or spareribs;
- no need to take the bones out as long as they fit into a common glass jar. The pieces should fit snugly in the jar;
- salt the meat as if you were going to fry it;
- have your salt all ready with one tablespoon of saltpeter and one of brown sugar to every teacupful of salt, all mixed well together;
- pack closely in your jars, pressing the meat down with a blunt stick about a foot long. An old sawed-off broom handle works well for this. Do not put any water into the jars;
- have a board full of holes to fit the bottom of your boiler;
- set the jars in and fill with warm water just to the caps;
- put on the caps but not the rubbers;
- let them stand until warm through;
- when warm, so they will not break, put on the stove and boil until done;
- it takes from an hour and a half to three hours, according to the age and kind of meat;
- to determine when it is done, take out a piece and taste it (simple as that);

- when done, set off the boiler;
- take out each jar and set it on a cloth to keep from breaking;
- in a few minutes, the juice will settle, and the jar will not be near full;
- have a pan of boiling saltwater ready, the same kind of salt used to salt the meat;
- keep it boiling and fill the jars full of saltwater and keep filling them as long as there is a bit of space;
- if you have used very fat meat, fill them so full that you run part of the fat off;
- when you are sure they are full, put on new rubbers and seal up as you would fruit;
- turn each can upside down to be sure it does not leak a drop. A leaking jar will let in air, and the meat will not keep;
- press the edge of the cap where there is a leak with the back of a knife or pound it a little with a small hammer.

Meat canned this way will keep almost any length of time and is nice to warm or to use cold. For breakfast, it can be floured and fried, and you can make gravy as you would with fresh fried meat. It works well to also use in making a meat pie.

As the next couple of years went by, we cleared more land, increased our supply of farm goods, and constructed new buildings or improved older ones.

We worked hard every day, except Sunday, to grow as much of our own food as we needed for each family household. We always tried to have extra of everything so we could sell some for cash or barter for those things we could not grow or make—things such as sugar, salt, coffee, or small farm tools.

By the time the Civil War broke out in April 1861, my family was getting along very well. We now had two households to support on our seventy acres of land since I had gotten married the previous year.

1860–1861

Weddings, cornhusking, pie socials, and family reunions were an important part of our mountain culture. At one such pie social held at the local picnic area by Laurel Run Creek on July 4, 1860, I noticed a pretty girl in a light-green dress. She was young—possibly nineteen or twenty—tall, and slender with a fine, sensitive face, beautiful dark eyes, and a scarlet mouth, like a leaf in a Tennessee autumn. Her hair was curled in tawny waves with little ringlets that framed her face.

She was already looking at me and shyly smiling in my direction. That moment was the beginning of a love affair that would last for the rest of our lives. From that point on, I was never interested in any other girl.

Her name was Amanda Jane Meek, and she was always on my mind. We got acquainted and met together as often as possible over the next several months. We went for many quiet walks alongside of Laurel Run Creek on our way up to the waterfalls, a hike of a little over two miles up and back. It is a beautiful, heavily wooded area. Regardless of the season, it was a great place for two young people to walk and talk about their hopes and dreams for the future. By nature, I was shy and guarded my emotions closely. But in meeting Amanda, I was enthralled by her warm, outgoing personality. I felt like I could confide my innermost thoughts and dreams with her. I knew someday we'd get married. Courtships didn't last long in those days, and we both realized we would make a good team and help each other build our lives together. Marriage just seemed right and natural.

So a few months later, on October 28, 1860, I married the love of my life. Jacob Hamilton, Justice of the Peace, performed the ceremony in the backyard of Amanda's parents' house, underneath a canopy of brilliant fall oak leaves.

A kindly gentleman, Mr. Hamilton was a man of authority and importance. Always elegantly dressed, he was a short, stout man with a bald head that rose majestically from broad, thick shoulders. He had a wide face that always seemed flushed, as if he spent most of his time outdoors. Mr. Hamilton had tiny restless eyes that looked like raisins stuck between two enormous pink ears. We loved Mr. Hamilton, and he had been a friend of the family since our arrival in Hawkins County.

Following our marriage, we set about carving out some land on my father's seventy acres and proceeded to enjoy a wonderful life together. With the help of my father and our wives, we built our log cabin with a huge stone chimney. I was a vigorous man standing five feet, eleven and a half inches tall, and the hard work of building our home was truly a labor of love for me. Amanda often said that I had a heart as warm as the large open fireplace in our home. She was so sweet.

At this time, however, the country was in a state of turmoil with the political environment heating up between the Northern and Southern states. Americans were forced to choose sides. Families were divided on the issue of slavery. Nobody was immune from the onslaught of the Civil War which erupted the following April 1861 at Fort Sumter in Charleston, South Carolina. Tennessee was the last state to withdraw from the Union in June 1861.

Regarding the question of slavery, I always believed it was a moral and political evil that had infected my country with divisiveness and hatred. My family had never owned slaves, and the neighbors I knew in Hawkins County did not participate in the institution of owning another fellow human being. Even though slavery had been a reality in many parts of the South for a long time, I felt that emancipation should be the result of the gentle welcoming arms of Christianity rather than the thunderous deadly arms of war. I would have been content to have remained neutral, given the choice.

1862

My older brother, John, whom I idolized, had migrated to Grayson County, Virginia, upon reaching adulthood. Grayson County is due west of Patrick County after passing through Carroll County. He was in search of work because, as I've said before, the old family farm was getting pretty crowded by this time. In Grayson County, John met a beautiful young lady named Mourning Hall. They were married on August 2, 1855, and began their family of three children. On our way to Hawkins County in 1856, we stopped and spent a few days with John and Mourning before continuing our journey west to Bays Mountain.

John and his family eventually moved to Hawkins County and were living here about sixteen months before his enlistment with Company A, Twelfth (Day's) Battalion, Tennessee Cavalry, Army of Tennessee on June 4, 1862, at Lyon's Store, Hawkins County. Captain Clinton D. Lyon was the organizer and later the commander of the company.

John's first engagement was Perryville, Kentucky. Confederate forces were trying to keep Tennessee as free of Federal control as possible, so a decision was made to "take the war to them" before they could gain the upper hand in our state. At this time, East Tennessee, where we lived, favored the Union but was under Confederate occupation. Middle and West Tennessee, which favored the Confederacy, was under Federal occupation. The control of eastern Tennessee was especially desired by President Lincoln because of the large number of Union sympathizers in our part of the state. The middle part of Tennessee was considered the most hostile war zone.

Prior to John's enlistment, Hawkins County donated the court-house bell to the Confederacy in April 1862. The bell was melted down and used in the making of bullets and cannonballs. Many local enlistees were greatly impressed by this gesture and prompted them to join the Confederacy.

When John enlisted, there was a great need to raise thousands of men to be mustered into the service of the Confederacy. Hundreds of state volunteers were enlisted or brought from nearby counties to join the cause. Most of these men were very ill equipped, and many of the state volunteers considered that they had to enter the ranks solely to protect their hearth and homes against invasion. At the urging of my brother, this argument about protecting our homes and property made sense to me, so I joined him later in the year.

I volunteered for service in the war at Knoxville, Tennessee, on Christmas Eve, 1862, along with my best friends, Porter Cavin and William Bowser. This was nearly twenty months after the war had begun in Charleston Harbor, South Carolina, on April 12, 1861.

I had known both Porter and William since coming to Hawkins County in 1856. They were descended from two families that had lived in the area for decades. We had known each other since our late teens, and now we were in our early twenties and faced with the prospect of a long and brutal war.

Porter was a strapping young man. Tall at six feet, three inches, he had a thick crest of ruddy hair, a broad full forehead, deep flashing brown eyes, a strong curved nose, high cheek bones, and a wide narrow mouth. Porter was a serious and thoughtful individual. He also had feet so large that the officer in charge of uniforms was concerned that he'd be able to find boots big enough to fit him!

William, on the other hand, had always seemed to be a delicately made child, but he grew up to be stocky and strong, finally topping out at a "commanding" five feet, eight inches. William had fine golden hair and a hesitant, charming smile punctuated by a dimple on his right cheek and a narrow heart-shaped birthmark on his left cheek. His nose was slightly tilted and somewhat patrician looking. Thick, fair eyebrows partially framed his pale-blue eyes. He had an air of playfulness and trust.

Together, Porter and William made a striking physical contrast, but both had the proclivity to speak quickly and act impetuously, which landed them in trouble more than once.

Before volunteering, Amanda and I had talked at length about what was best for us. She tried to discourage me from enlisting by saying that I was more needed on the farm than on the battlefield. As members of the Dunkard Brethren, we were opposed to war, believing what Jesus said in John 18:36 when He explained the nature of His kingdom. He told his disciples that he had no political motives in mind and that His kingdom is a spiritual one which is not built, nor is it maintained, by military might.

Some thought the war would not last much longer, but in the end, we both felt the need to take a stand against outside invaders. I was able to enlist to do the work of a blacksmith and teamster so I would not be involved, directly, in the killing of another human being.

During most of this time of discussing our future, Amanda was pregnant with our first child. We welcomed Elizabeth Francis into the world on September 8, 1862, but our little darling girl blessed us for only twenty days before she succumbed to pneumonia on September 28, 1862. We were heartbroken and drew upon each other and the Lord to sustain us through that extremely difficult time. We will never know the reason why Elizabeth was taken from us, and even if we did, it would not have lessened the pain. We knew only the Lord could give us relief from that pain.

Along with Porter and William, I was assigned to the same unit as brother John—Company A, Twelfth Battalion, Tennessee Cavalry, Army of Tennessee—as a stock hand, teamster, and blacksmith.

That doesn't sound overly exciting, but due to my opposition to war, it did keep me out of the thick of most battles during the next two and a half years. Porter and William were assigned to the infantry and served with John.

Often overlooked, the skills of a blacksmith served a key role in helping maintain an efficient mobile army. I was usually behind the battle lines but certainly not out of danger. My job was to drive the wagons with supplies, fix the wagons when they needed to be repaired, and tend to the mules and horses. Attached to my supply wagon was a limber, which is a two-wheeled cart designed to support a traveling forge, allowing it to be towed. The traveling forge was basically a blacksmith's shop on wheels which consisted of a bellows attached to a fireplace, a 4-inch-wide vise, a 100-pound anvil, and a box containing 250 pounds of coal, 200 pounds of horseshoes, and 4-foot-long bundles of iron bars; and on the limber was a box containing my blacksmith's tools. The limber could be easily unhooked so as not to slow down the delivery of supplies. I had everything I needed to fix wagons, shoe horses, and just about anything else that might come up in the course of a day.

Armies need weapons, food, and other supplies. An army must carry these supplies to use daily because an army without supplies is an army unable to fight. They are carried in supply trains made up of wagons, horses, mules, and teamsters, who drove the wagons. In addition to my being a blacksmith, I was also a teamster.

A teamster is a soldier whose job is extremely dirty and dangerous. When my wagon was empty, I had to go back to the supply base to reload and return to the battle or camp. I had to reload my wagon with the same type of supplies that I had carried before. Our wagons were marked to note the contents: ammunition, supplies, or whatever if for infantry or artillery; if forage, whether grain or hay; and if rations, whether bread, pork, beans, rice, sugar, coffee, or whatever it might be. Empty wagons were never allowed to follow the army or stay in camp. As soon as a wagon was empty, it would return to the supply base for a load of the same material that had been previously emptied. Empty wagon trains were ordered to leave the road open for loaded ones.

In my case, I hauled ammunition; so when I was empty, I made a return trip to get more ammunition from the supply base, which was oftentimes miles away.

As far as the South was concerned, our supply systems broke down on a regular basis. Unlike the North, we did not have the iron needed to repair damaged railroad tracks and thus had to rely on wagon trains to haul the supplies necessary to keep our battalion armed and fed. It seemed I was always repairing wagon wheels and axles. Horses also died pulling wagons, exhausted from heavy loads, and we would have to contend with that little problem as well. As the war continued, the shortage of horses and wagons became more severe, leaving military commanders with starving Confederate soldiers and starving Federal prisoners. Hardly any fruit or vegetables were available, and scurvy was an ever-present danger. Privation was considered the normal state of existence. The prevailing military thinking at the time was privation kept the troops focused on imminent battles. I always thought I could focus just as well with a full belly. But no one asked me.

The Twelfth Battalion, Tennessee Cavalry, Army of Tennessee was formed in mid-1862 with four companies, later increased to seven. Its members were raised in Hawkins, Greene, Knox, Hamblen, and Grainger Counties.

Over the course of the Civil War, the Twelfth Battalion was assigned to Wharton's, Morrison's, Davidson's, Grigsby's, and Vaughn's brigades. It fought at Perryville, Kentucky, where my brother was first engaged in battle and then later at Murfreesboro, Chattanooga, Chickamauga, Mission Ridge, and Piedmont.

Because I had not volunteered until December 1862, I missed the Twelfth Battalion's engagement at Perryville, Kentucky, which took place on October 8, 1862. This campaign was also known as the Confederate Heartland Offensive. The principal commanders were Major General Don Buell (Federal) and Major General Braxton Bragg (Confederate).

Major General Braxton Bragg had begun an invasion of Kentucky in early fall 1862. He made it as far as the outskirts of Louisville when he was forced to retreat and regroup at Perryville, Kentucky. On October 7, the Federal Army, numbering roughly 55,000 troops, converged at the small crossroads town to confront the Confederate cavalry. Skirmishing was brisk; but because additional Federal reinforcements were threatening to overwhelm Bragg's army, and his being short of men and supplies, he withdrew during the night and continued his retreat by way of the Cumberland Gap into eastern Tennessee. A quick ride on horseback on Christmas Day was required for me to assist in the battle at Murfreesboro, which is the exact geographic center of Tennessee. This is when I caught up with the Twelfth Battalion and a homecoming with John. Arriving just in time, I was assigned to my own wagon and limber shortly before the battle began on December 31, 1862.

Upon arriving, I was told that after General Bragg's defeat at Perryville, Kentucky, on October 8, he and his Confederate Army retreated to Nashville, reorganized, and prepared to go into their winter quarters at Murfreesboro. However, Major General William S. Rosecrans, who had replaced Buell, and his Federal Army had other plans.

Rosecrans's Federal Army of the Cumberland had followed Bragg's army from Kentucky to Nashville and caught up with us at Murfreesboro on December 29, well within hearing distance of our troops. In fact, just across the river, you could see the Federal campfires set in the low valleys of the distant hills. This was my first encounter with the Federal Army, and many thoughts ran through my mind. I'd had no training after my enlistment but was simply told to catch up with Bragg's army and do whatever teamsters and blacksmiths do.

I was well behind the lines with my supply wagon and black-smith's limber when Rosecrans's army arrived, but I was deeply concerned for brother John. He was on the front lines, and the little time I'd had to talk to him in the last couple of days revealed that he had been detailed to hazardous and special task vidette duty. A vidette is a mounted sentinel posted in advance of the outposts of an army. The duty of a vidette is to watch with the strictest attention the movements of the Federal troops if such troops are within range of his vision. Also, he is to listen for the least noise and notice the smallest incident which could be of importance to the picket or detachment that sent him out.

Rosecrans's army had encamped close enough that John was able to observe and hear almost everything that was going on from his distance. He reported what he had learned to his superiors, and at dawn on December 31, we attacked the Federal right flank. Fierce fighting ensued, and we were able to drive their line back to the Nashville Pike by midmorning. But our advance stalled there.

Meanwhile, supplies were needed at the front, so I spent the morning of New Year's Eve driving to and from the supply depot with loads of ammunition for our troops. I could hear the fighting from about a mile away. The noise was constant and thunderous. I unloaded my crates of ammunition at a designated spot in territory that our troops had taken from the enemy. Already, bodies were piling up along with horses, mules, and broken wagons. Whole groves of trees had been shattered and leveled by cannon fire. The smoke from the battle lay heavy and acrid across the landscape. The mind can only absorb so much of what it is not used to, and then it tends to go numb. That was the case with me. It was a surreal picture, and I stumbled through the remainder of the morning and into the early afternoon trying to focus on the supplies needed by our troops.

Late in the afternoon, Federal reinforcements arrived to bolster their ranks; and before the fighting had stopped for the day, the Federal forces had established a strong new line of defense.

1863

The following day, New Year's Day, 1863, there were minor skirmishes; but no intense fighting took place.

Bragg thought that Rosecrans would now withdraw; but that was not to be the case because, the next morning, he was still in position. Late in the afternoon, Bragg decided to throw one of his divisions at a Federal division that had crossed the Stones River on New Year's Day. This division had taken up a strong position on the bluff east of the river. Our troops drove most of the Federal troops back across McFadden's Ford. But then with the aid of Federal artillery, our attack was stopped, and we had to fall back to our original position.

I wandered through the camp on the evening of January 2 looking for John. After inquiring of his whereabouts, I found him propped up against the stump of what was left of a huge oak tree just about the time that a torrential downpour began. I was so overwhelmed to see he had survived the Murfreesboro battle that, despite the rain, we caught each other up in a big bear hug. He had cuts and bruises here and there but, for the most part, was in good shape. He was in dire need of water, so I shared what I had in my canteen and a little hard tack to eat.

With our tents being full of gravely wounded comrades, John and I sat against the tree stump through most of the night in a torrential downpour. We were miserable on the outside but warm on the inside because, as brothers, we had survived together to see another break of dawn.

We had sat and talked for about an hour until John fell back, completely exhausted, into a deep sleep. I held his hand and said a little prayer of thanks to the Lord for protecting us during this battle. I knew I had some work to do on the broken wagons in the morning, so I tried my best to get some much-needed rest knowing that my work was cut out for me. Rumors were flying around the encampment that we were retreating; and that meant the wagons had to be repaired, horses reshod, and camp broken down so we could move out.

Since the Federal Army had been strongly reinforced, Bragg did, in fact, decide that retreating would be the wisest choice. On January 4 and 5, we packed up our army and retreated to Shelbyville and Tullahoma, Tennessee. Winter conditions were harsh; and Rosecrans, as Bragg had suspected, did not pursue.

General Rosecrans, with a reputation for bold action, succumbed to caution on his way to Chattanooga and kept his army in place, occupying Murfreesboro for almost six months. After defeating Bragg and our army at Stones River, he just suddenly stopped. They spent that time resupplying and training, but Rosecrans was also hesitant to advance toward us on the muddy winter roads that we had just used, leaving them in even worse condition. The entire face of the country looked like a bog.

Our encampment in the Shelbyville and Tullahoma area suffered from the delays. Not only was our retreat during winter conditions, but we occupied a location known as the Barrens. This proved to be an accurate name because it was extremely poor farmland that made it difficult for us to obtain needed food, supplies, and other resources for our army. All of this was occurring while waiting for the imminent attack by Rosecrans's army.

It is ironic that while we were stationed in this area for the protection of farm supplies of the South moving by rail through Chattanooga, we were close to starving. We discovered that large amounts of those supplies were being shipped east to General Robert E. Lee's Army of Northern Virginia. Our unit, on the other hand, had to exist on a daily ration of four ounces of bacon or salt pork, with only one pint of cornmeal per man. The shortage of food and supplies for our men also meant shortages of feed for our livestock. Such shortages led to slow starvation for the horses and loss of livestock through hunger and disease. I had heard reports that over half of the animals in some horse artillery units had died.

After our retreat from Murfreesboro, our army, still under the command of General Bragg, occupied a strong defensive position in the mountains. I spent my time during those cold winter months and early spring days fixing wagons, repairing cannon wheels, making sure the horses were reshod, and just trying to survive.

The winter of early 1863 brought more rain than usual causing flooding in the few dry places where we sought to pitch our tents. Our battalion had set up camp in the nearest fields and pastures around Shelbyville and Tullahoma. It didn't take long for our tents to spring up like weeds in the early spring. Campfires soon followed, and they glowed a deep red that dotted the night, revealing our army stretched out for miles on the open land.

For me, in my own quiet moments at night, my mind wandered back to Hawkins County where I knew Amanda waited for me. Thankfully, these memories momentarily replaced the stench of horse manure and the smell of my blacksmith's forge. Time and time again, day after day, I was reminded that this war now promised to be long, brutal, and soul scarring.

It did not take long for me to feel a great pity for myself. I wished longingly that I was home with Amanda once again doing such simple tasks as the farm chores. I had pleasant memories of walking from our cabin to the livestock shed, then out to our small fields of crops, back from the fields to the livestock shed, and from the livestock shed to our cabin. I swore I would never take those simple times for granted ever again.

To rise out of my self-imposed pity, I would often seek out Porter and William. Occasionally, we would be joined by our young drummer boy, Johnny McKinney, who hailed from Grainger County. We had nicknamed him Johnny Cadence—or for short, just plain Cadence—because of his perfect rhythmic beat to keep the infantry in step as they marched toward a pending battle. There's nothing quite like a good drum line to fire up the troops. Johnny Cadence was about fifteen years old. Soft spoken and polite, Cadence had a quickness and eagerness to please his elders. With blond hair and piercing blue eyes, he had a quiet, reserved nature that belied his courage in the face of an oncoming charge of Federal troops.

Also joining us from time to time was Dustin "Dusty" Odom, an artillery man from neighboring Greene County. I had gotten to know him while repairing a wheel part on his artillery piece. Dusty had dark close-cropped hair, large hands, and a high forehead. He was blessed with a deep, hearty laugh that started in his barrel chest and reverberated throughout his six-foot-two-inch frame all the way to his size 14 feet. Serious and thoughtful in nature, Dusty was always ready to lighten the atmosphere with a good joke.

We would often talk long into the night of our hopes and dreams when the war ended. Without it being said, there was always the underlying thought that we could all be killed. No one ever talked about it, but it lingered in the air like the gray smoke from our campfire.

At other times, to keep up morale, I was called upon to lead prayers around the campfires at night. Some in my battalion had seen me reading my Bible at night and had noticed my quiet demeanor amidst the chaos of battle. It was at night, in the relative silence, when you could still smell the gunpowder and sweat mixed with the thick air of battle that men's souls cried out for the comfort and peace only God can give.

Armed with my squirrel skin-covered Bible which I carried in my knapsack, I would wander through the rows of hungry, tired, and wounded men to see if I could be of comfort to any of them. Those who were not sleeping would grab my arm or pant leg and ask for a personal prayer. I would kneel, hold their hand, and pray for them to return safely to loved ones back home. Some prayers called for quick healing of wounds of the body and mind as they wrestled with the horrors of a seemingly never-ending war. Their minds were tormented at night by the images of men blown apart by a fuselage of cannonballs or seeing their friends bayoneted in hand-to-hand combat as they lay helpless, pleading for their lives.

At the end of such days, totally exhausted, I would return to my sleeping cot and stare into the night as the glow from the campfire gradually dimmed on the yellowed walls of my tent.

And then, by Divine Providence, for I could not explain it any other way, just when I was at the lowest depths of despair, I would receive a letter from Amanda.

April 15, 1863

My dearest beloved husband,

This quiet evening, you are on my heart. I pray that you are safe and are taking care of yourself. I do not know exactly where you are. Some of the neighbors say that you are around the Shelbyville area, and if so, I hope the army mail catches up with you. I know the Lord is watching over you, and that comforts me. I hope this war will not last very long and you will be returned safely to the warmth of our home.

All is well on our little farm. Several of the neighbor boys have been helping me with the few chickens, hogs, and cows that we have. I hope someday we will have a house full of our own children so that we can, together, watch them grow. As I think about children, I am always reminded of our little Elizabeth and the short life she had last September. Then, this war took you away from me. Yes, I remember our long talks about how your service to protect our home would help us in the long run, and I am thankful for your sacrifice for me and our future. You are a good man, Green. The day you left, I felt that I had given my best to the country I love, and I kept my tears inside until you were gone.

It is getting late, and Hazel needs to get back to her own family over in the next holler. She is so kind to write these letters for me as I tell her what I want to say to you. I wished I had learned to write back when I was younger, but the schooling just wasn't there. Besides, Hazel has such pretty writing.

I will be going to sleep in a little while, but I know when I awake, you will be the sun in my sky. Early tomorrow morning when I draw water from the well, I will think of you as the river that runs through my soul. And tomorrow night, as I stand on the front porch, breathing the sweetness of spring, you are the very air that I breathe.

Good night, darling. Before I met you, I didn't believe it was possible to love someone so deeply and completely. But you have given me faith that true love really does exist because I share it with you.

All my love,
Amanda

*****

June 14, 1863

My dearest Amanda,

I am sitting alone in my tent tonight. My thoughts are of you. I received your letter dated April 15, and I carry it in my breast pocket next to my heart. That is where you will always be. I have a lot to catch up on with you since I have been on the move constantly.

Since I volunteered last December, the Twelfth Cavalry has been involved in several battles and skirmishes. Shortly after I left you, I made a hurried ride to Murfreesboro and caught up with the Twelfth. Brother John was very happy to see me, and since then, we've spent many hours in front of campfires talking about home. I worry a lot about John because he is a mounted sentinel on the frontlines, truly in harm's way. I pray daily for his safety.

As for me, the things I learned blacksmithing and taking care of stock have really helped our unit to stay in good shape. The work is constant.

We got routed at Murfreesboro and have since retreated to Shelbyville and Tullahoma. It was the dead of the winter, and the roads were mud pits. I followed in the supply train and mended wagons or helped pull them out of the mud when they got stuck.

Conditions are very bad. We need food and supplies. On top of that, the generals have received word that Rosecrans and his army left Murfreesboro a few weeks back, so we are expecting an attack at any time.

The weather looks like it could rain for days. Sure hope not. We are in bad enough shape. Well, my dearest, it is getting late; and tomorrow promises to be more of the same. I wish I could be with you, but better we fight the enemy here rather than on our farm.

The last time I saw John, he asked me to pass on his love to his lovely wife. I trust that Mourning and their three children are doing well. Let me know in a future letter, and I will pass that along to John. He sends his greetings to you, as well. Also, give my best to Hazel. She writes very well, but it is your words that comfort

me. Please have her write as often as she can, and
I hope your letters catch up with me.

Good night, my love. I am...

Forever yours,
Green

When the weather turned warmer, we knew that Rosecrans's army would be on the move; and sure enough, in early June 1863, we were told to prepare for battle. However, a great rainstorm that began on June 24 did not stop until July 4. Brother John told me later that his entire unit was soaked to the skin and roughly nine out of ten rifles were too wet to shoot. The rains considerably slowed down Rosecrans's entire offensive, but through a series of excellent military maneuvers and aided by the newly introduced seven-shot Spencer rifle, Rosecrans captured several key passes.

All the while, tensions were running high in our camp. Ever since Bragg's Kentucky campaign at the Battle of Perryville and Murfreesboro, his subordinate generals were nearly mutinous in expressing their dissatisfaction with his command.

In early June, the Twelfth and the Sixteenth Battalions were consolidated into a new field organization known as Rucker's Legion. Battalions were often consolidated as casualties mounted during the war to present larger commands to the enemy.

Because of the dissension between our generals, Rosecrans's occupation of the key mountain passes, and a lack of supplies, we were forced out of our previous strong position on the morning of June 27 and had to abandon our headquarters at Shelbyville and, a few days later, at Tullahoma.

As July 3 dawned, a heavy mist hung over the land. We were rousted from our sleep because General Bragg had ordered a retreat to Chattanooga, a strategic city located at the juncture of Tennessee, Alabama, and Georgia. It held the key to future forays into Georgia and Virginia. Nestled in a valley between the Appalachian and Cumberland mountain ranges, Chattanooga was a rail hub for three railroads and thus was a particularly important site for both armies.

We broke camp and began a slow march along a narrow road that led deep into the woods. Our column stretched for miles and was very scattered. The soldiers who still carried their muskets barely looked like fighting men as they wearily tramped along with tattered clothes, sunken eyes, and faces pale and pinched. The team of mules I was driving was already half-starved and ready to collapse as they strained to pull the heavy ordnance wagon, which seemed to groan under the weight. We crossed the Tennessee River on July 4, and by July 7, all Confederate units had encamped near Lookout Mountain. It was well known that whoever controlled the 1,200-foot-high Lookout Mountain controlled the major routes into Chattanooga.

Our generals correctly figured that Rosecrans would probably start a renewed offensive in his quest to drive us out of Chattanooga. By early September, Rosecrans had consolidated his forces that had been scattered in Tennessee and Georgia and, after heavy fighting, was successful in forcing us out of Chattanooga.

From there, we headed south to Chickamauga, fifteen miles southeast of Chattanooga in the hill country of Northwest Georgia. John's unit was among the first to see action after they had advanced from their camp near Alexander's Bridge. Soon after daylight, on September 9, John's unit attacked Croxton's brigade of Brannon's division at Jay's Sawmill. The fighting was fierce, and we were forced to retreat. The Federal troops followed, and our cavalries briefly skirmished at Davis's Cross Roads on September 15. General Bragg was determined to reoccupy Chattanooga; so on September 17, we headed back north intending to meet, and defeat, the XXI Army Corps. Late in the afternoon on the eighteenth, our cavalry and infantry fought with Federal cavalry and mounted infantry, which were, once again, armed with the deadly Spencer repeating rifles. The heaviest fighting began on the morning of the nineteenth as our cavalry, infantry, and artillery repeatedly pounded away at the Federal line. However, it did not break.

The next day, the twentieth, in a surprise attack at Chickamauga Creek, we threw everything we had at the Federal line's left flank. Our infantry, rushing forward in thickly wooded terrain with Porter and William joining in the now famous high-pitched rebel yell, succeeded in creating a gap in the line. Fifteen thousand Confederate troops charged through this gap. When Rosecrans attempted to fill this gap by moving other units around, he created an even bigger gap which was quickly exploited by General James Longstreet, who had been dispatched by General Robert E. Lee to assist the Army of Tennessee in driving the Federal forces back. Though strongly contested, the Battle of Chickamauga was a significant victory for the Confederacy. Rosecrans was badly defeated with a heavy loss of artillery. Our forces, including John, Porter, and William, succeeded in driving the Federals back to Chattanooga where we took possession of Missionary Ridge to the east and Lookout Mountain to the west, both overlooking Chattanooga. Rosecrans had abandoned both Missionary Ridge and Lookout Mountain and, in so doing, his control of the river and river road as far back as Bridgeport. Because of our victory at Chickamauga, hope rose in every Southern heart.

When I caught up with John at midmorning on the twenty-first, I had never seen him look this way. He had been in the thick of the assault at Chickamauga. His eyes appeared hollow, unseeing, as if total exhaustion had wrenched every fiber of his body. Only when I knelt to where he was huddled near a supply wagon did he appear to even recognize me. We just stared at each other for a few minutes before either of us spoke. Finally, his eyes brightened a little bit, and he reached out his hand for mine. We shared a drink of water from my canteen and a little bit of salt pork. In a few minutes, his spirits seemed restored, and we talked about the battle over the last few days. We both felt that if we could follow up this victory, our whole gloomy existence might just be changed for the better. However, our jubilation over the victory lasted only a few days. Our entire army, exhausted by the effort to win this battle, were forced to simply occupy the surrounding heights, of Lookout Mountain and Missionary Ridge, where John took up his post.

Lookout Mountain and Missionary Ridge overlook the town of Chattanooga. By occupying these strategic locations, our army blocked almost all supply routes. Our army commanded the railroad, the river, and the shortest and best wagon roads, both south and north of the Tennessee River, between Chattanooga and Bridgeport.

The distance between these two cities is about twenty-six miles by rail; but because of our occupation of these strategic positions, we knew that all supplies for Federal troops had to be hauled by a much longer route north of the river and over mountainous country, increasing the distance to over sixty miles.

General Bragg was convinced that the Federal forces in the town would soon be starved into surrender. Because Chattanooga was such an important railroad station, we figured the Federal response to their situation would be swift and overpowering. They had the resources to do this, but they had to get them to Chattanooga. About this time, it was rumored that Jefferson Davis had visited Bragg on Missionary Ridge a short time before the battle began. It was reported and believed that he had come out to reconcile a serious rift between Bragg and Longstreet.

We learned that Federal reinforcements were being rushed to the Chattanooga area from the east and the west. We had cavalry units that were trying to intercept these troops and supply trains while they were en route. Supplies from Nashville that were headed south to relieve Chattanooga were destroyed on October 5 near Murfreesboro by General Joe Wheeler and his Confederate cavalry. He also blew up the railroad which created a serious problem for the city. Because we did not control Walden's Ridge, a high point to the northwest of Chattanooga, the Federals attempted to use that pass as a supply route. This proved disastrous for them as Wheeler hit a Federal wagon train on the Ridge, chasing off or killing the teamsters and killing the mules. Our forces were determined to maintain a blockade of Chattanooga, but killing a good mule just didn't seem right to me! I mean, heck, a mule doesn't care which side it's on! I suppose they were just following orders. Who was I to say anything, but it just seemed like we could have saved the mules since many of ours had been killed and were dying by the dozens. Both sides had little to no forage, but the Federal forces trapped inside the city had the short end of the deal. If they lost their animals, it would pin them in Chattanooga even if they broke the siege.

During most of October, as small battles and skirmishes took place, the Federal forces, now under control of General U. S. Grant, had devised a plan to build what was called a cracker line. This was a winding supply route through territory they occupied and proved to be the saving grace for their forces. Once the cracker line was completed, supplies began flowing into Chattanooga, and we could do little to stop them.

At first, the rations were brought through Lookout Valley once our soldiers had been driven out of the area. These rations were mostly made up of hardtack and dried beef. Cracker is a nickname for hardtack, and that is where the name *cracker line* came into being.

After we were driven off Lookout Mountain, that left Missionary Ridge as the only Confederate stronghold; and, unfortunately, that is where brother John was posted. Although only three hundred feet high, Missionary Ridge's steep slopes gave the dug-in defenders a huge advantage against attackers. This ridge was heavily fortified with three lines of trenches: one at the base, one halfway up, and one at the top. John was in the top trench.

It had rained constantly on the days of November 20 and 21. The roads were nearly impassable from the knee-deep mud and the washouts on the mountain sides. The roads were filled with broken wagons and the carcasses of thousands of starved mules and horses.

This did not stop the Federal forces. With thousands of reinforcements pouring into the area, it did not take long for a force to be assembled and head toward Missionary Ridge. At 1:00 a.m. on November 24, the Federal assault began on Missionary Ridge. Because of the heavy rain earlier in the week, the clouds were so low that Lookout Mountain and the top of Missionary Ridge were impossible to see from the valley. Our forces did not seem to be aware of Federal troop movement in the valley until it was too late, and they had quickly breached the first entrenchments at the lower level of the mountain. Once the attack began, seriously outnumbered and hampered by the heavy fog, our soldiers panicked, broke ranks, and fled up the hill. By doing this, our men in the second trench were restricted from firing on the Federal troops pursuing them, lest they shoot our own men. Men in the second trench, seeing what was happening, also fled up the hill until those that survived tried vainly to put up a fight on top. After an hour of heavy fighting, Federal troops reached the top of Missionary Ridge, and the route was on. By 3:15 p.m., Federal forces were in control of the height.

While all of this was going on, I was miles away in the wagon supply line waiting for orders to assist our troops should the fighting go our way. I could hear the constant roar of artillery and small-arms fire for several hours.

I was fifty yards away and mostly out of danger, or so I thought, when suddenly and unexpectedly, an errant Federal shell came screaming out of nowhere over the road on which I was resting my team and slammed into one of our supply wagons that had been pulled to the side of the road. The shell was a three-inch rifled Parrott, weighing nearly ten pounds and made with an impact fuse. It struck just above the wagon's left front wheel at an angle toward the back of the wagon bed. The immediate explosion, combined with the force of impact, blew the wagon, the mules, and everything in it to pieces. Fortunately, it was not an ammunition wagon like the one I was sitting on, but rather it was loaded with food supplies. The impact and explosion blew me off the wagon seat, nearly deafened me, and rained down food supplies, wood, metal, and various mule parts all around me.

I regained my composure after a few minutes and assessed any damage to my wagon. Seeing none, I remounted the seat and waited for orders. It was now nearly 4:00 p.m., and the fighting had slackened.

With Federal forces in control on Missionary Ridge, the only choice our soldiers had was to make a hasty retreat down the mountain into some relative safety. Just enough of our army remained intact to protect the retreat of our soldiers. John escaped safely and joined the retreat. His unit was coming down a narrow, steep mountain path when I spotted him in the distance shortly after 4:00 p.m. The long line of ragged men streamed toward me through the mud. There were some men so weak that they could barely keep up with the column and they were beginning to straggle behind.

I knew which one was John, but as he shuffled toward me, he did not look the same. It was obvious he was worn out from the battle, his uniform dirty and torn.

John told me, when we met up, that it was a complete disaster on top of the ridge. He described the forest at the top of Missionary Ridge as seeming to shake and grow larger from the rifle firing and the rushing Federal forces, who seemed to be running at them from every direction. Many Confederate soldiers were already lying dead and dying in the mud. John said they tried to make a skirmish line on the ridge, but General Bragg had placed only a lightly defended far-right position. Before they knew it, Federal soldiers came streaming out of the woods, spreading rapidly forward. They halted, formed a line of battle, and began sweeping directly at them. They were so close that he could see their smudged faces with varying degrees of blackness from the burned powder of their muskets. At this time, John said, he could hear the bugles blasting and orders being shouted. Retreat was the only option.

John and I had just a few minutes to talk as they came by. He spoke haltingly, having to measure each word as if his mouth could not say what his eyes had seen up on the ridge. He told me that even though he had survived this battle, he had a sense of foreboding that his luck was going to run out one of these days. The odds were against him, he said. I tried to reassure him that everything was going to be all right and as soon as he got to safety, he needed to get some rest and next morning would be better. I did not realize it at the time, but John's words were prophetic. I never saw him again.

After the fighting was over, I was assigned to get as close as I could to the battleground and salvage whatever still looked useful and load it into an empty wagon while my one full of ammunition went with our retreating army by another teamster. After we had spoken for a few minutes and John had marched on, I was left to my job.

As I approached the scene in front of me, it unfolded and looked like a nightmare from hell. The carnage was horrific. It stunned my mind and overwhelmed my senses. What hours before had been living, breathing men was now a field of battered, shattered, and scattered human remains. Everywhere there were arms, legs, and headless bodies whose gray coats appeared to be partially dyed black, evidence of the shed blood of young men. Their weapons and their personal keepsakes were scattered like trash blown in the wind. Caps, knapsacks, playing cards, and small pocket Bibles were strewn about, a last testament to that instant of time when believers are transported from the here and now, into Eternity.

The defeat at Missionary Ridge on November 25 secured Federal control of Chattanooga and, with that, control of East Tennessee. At this time, Rucker's Legion was placed in Colonel J. Warren Grigsby's brigade, Brigadier General John H. Kelly's division of Major General Joseph Wheeler's cavalry corps, and detached with Lieutenant General Longstreet on orders to move into East Tennessee. This is when John and I were separated. He was assigned to another cavalry unit because of his special vidette duty experience and, after licking their wounds, headed south to Dalton, Georgia, a distance of 32 miles.

The defeat at Chattanooga, coming at the end of the year, handed the initiative for 1864 to the Federal forces. At this time, though, both armies spent the winter of 1863–1864 within eyesight and earshot of each other with no confrontations. The only major occurrence at this time happened up north in Hawkins County when Federal soldiers broke into the courthouse and seized hundreds of records and burned them on the courthouse square to keep warm. Many records dating back to 1765 were destroyed.

Federal forces now had control over most of the battle theaters, and they were in a strong position to aim their attacks toward the Confederate capital in Richmond. We were all cold, wet, and hungry. It was an intensely cold winter as the thermometer plunged down as low as zero every morning for a week. I agonized over the men who shivered in their half nakedness or stained the road with shoeless, bleeding feet.

Word was now going around the various camps that the Confederate government had only twenty-five day's supply of beef and bacon east of the Mississippi River and had no reserves whatsoever in Virginia. The constant refrain in our unit was about "sore feet and short rations." At times, I was sent out to forage for food and supplies from sympathetic folks in the countryside. They sacrificed and gave what they could from their gardens, fields, and smokehouses. However, at times, I had to refuse what was offered after peering into the starving faces of the women and children. There were no men around except for an occasional elderly man who would simply stare straight ahead from his rocking chair on the rickety front porch. Most times, the land had already been stripped.

Religion was an important factor in sustaining the spirit of our army through the long winter months. During this particular winter, hundreds of men were converted with a faith that defied the battle for survival. I was called upon to tend to the spiritual needs of the men. We held small prayer meetings around the campfires during most evenings, and on Sundays, it was a time for larger nondenominational services along with other activities to lighten the burden of camp life. Even with all of this, I did not feel like it was going to be a happy New Year. And then, another letter from Amanda arrived.

November 19, 1863

My dearest husband,

I received your last letter dated June 14, written nearly five months ago. The mail is traveling so slowly. We are hearing that many of the railroad tracks have been blown up, so this is probably the reason why.

Hazel and I have been talking for most of the evening. She came over for supper so that we could visit a little bit before sitting down to write this letter to you.

I must confess, Green, that I have a chill in my heart tonight. Even though I have started a warm fire in our fireplace, there is a coldness in the air that has nothing to do with the early fall weather.

The news we are hearing is not good. There is a lot of talk about terrible fighting in Murfreesboro, Chickamauga, and Chattanooga.

We know that both you and John are in those places, and we constantly pray for you.

Mourning and I have gotten together several times to swap news that we have heard. It sounds like we are losing at every turn except for the short victory at Chickamauga. Closer to home, there has been talk that some folks around here that are loyal to the Union have burned several bridges on the Holston River, including the big one west of here at Strawberry Plains. I believe it was burned just this past June. It seems the war has gotten a lot closer. Please be careful, Green. I need you to come home safely. You and John both.

We celebrated my twenty-third birthday a few weeks ago. Some of the neighbor ladies came over, and we had shortcakes and coffee. It was just not the same without you. Mrs. Bowser and Mrs. Cavin were here and said they don't know anything about their boys. We know they are in your company, so next time you write, please pass along any news you might have about them. You have known each other a long time, so we hope all is well with the men from Hawkins County. We are proud of all of you, and just remember that you are in our prayers daily. I must close now, Green. It is terribly lonely around here without you. Winter will be coming soon, and I dread this time of year. But thoughts of you and your safe homecoming has warmed my heart.

All my love,
Amanda

1864

On January 31, 1864, my legion totaled 171 effectives. In January and February, we were on the move around Russellville and other points such as Sneedville, Mooresburg, Chucky Bend, Morristown, Strawberry Plains, New Market, and Dandridge. On February 29, Rucker's Legion was disbanded and transferred to Dibrell's division and Vaughn's brigade. Desertion was becoming a disease. The reasons were many: hunger, delayed pay, and the awareness that the general public was growing numb to the war. But probably the main reason for desertion was the woeful letters that some men received from wives and families telling of the danger or privation at home.

We seemed to be constantly on the move with many stops and difficult travel. Camp life often evolved into weeks of boredom, but I was usually busy with my work of repairs and livestock care. Even so, I did find a little time to write to Amanda. I was desperate to know how things were going back home.

February 27, 1864

Dearest beloved Amanda,

Your letter of November 19 of last year has caught up with me. Your words always comfort me. I treasure them and read them often, especially at night. I miss you so much.

We have been moving around for months now, trying to stay ahead of Federal forces. Please tell Mrs. Cavin and Mrs. Bowser that both Porter and William are okay, even though all of us are feeling the pinch of short rations. Hopefully, this will put their minds at ease knowing their boys are alive. I guess Porter and William just don't like to write, so I will do my best to keep everyone informed.

Talk is going around that we might be headed into the Valley of Virginia to begin a campaign there. This war just seems to go on and on. We are outnumbered by the Federal troops and have fewer supplies and guns. I don't know how we can keep going. We have also lost many of our best officers in battle. My hands hurt all the time from the repair work needed to keep our supply trains moving and the horses shoed. I can't wait for the time when all the steel and metal wasted in this war can be melted down into plowshares. That would be a much better use for it rather than the killing of men.

Well, my love, it is getting late; and the mules and horses must be fed and watered. The work never ends, but at least I can go to sleep tonight knowing you are safe and have the comfort of family, friends, and neighbors close by. I am content knowing, God willing, I will return to you. I am tired of this war and being separated from you. In the meantime, sleep well.

Good night, my love. I am…

Forever yours,
Green

On April 29, 1864, my Twelfth Battalion had 234 men due to further consolidation as we moved into the Valley of Virginia. On June 5, we were engaged in a renewed Federal offensive north of

Piedmont. The battle was fierce and furious as our armies, totaling thousands on both sides, fought in the hills—dense forests of scrub oak, pine, and willows of what once had been a peaceful place. I could hear the artillery and infantry firing away at each other from the seat on my supply wagon. I had been busy for weeks laying in supplies, guns, and ammunition for what many thought was going to be a major battle.

However, the battle was short lived as the Federal forces made several successful flanking movements which caught our troops completely off guard. Our leader, "Grumble" Jones, while trying to stop our forces from retreating, was killed. At that point, the retreat became a rout. In front of me, I caught a glimpse of a road in the distance, winding over the low-lying hills. It was choked with our retreating infantry. Furthermore, more than 1,000 of our troops, including 60 officers, were captured. In addition, we lost three long-range cannons. We could ill afford such losses of men and equipment. We barely had time to regroup and limp back toward the Tennessee border.

On the way back, word trickled down that the most important railroad bridge in East Tennessee, the 1,600-foot-long bridge at Strawberry Plains, had been destroyed in an artillery duel between our forces and the Federals. It was the only bridge supporting the rail lines in that area which made it a priority target for Federal forces. It had exchanged hands several times over the years as one side would destroy it and the other side would rebuild it.

Because of our losses at Piedmont, the Twelfth and Sixteenth Battalions were merged into the First Tennessee Cavalry Regiment in late August. We were near Bristol in September and Kingsport in October. On October 18, we engaged in a brutal skirmish with the Second Federal Tennessee Regiment in Grainger County.

In December, we settled into our winter quarters near Thorn Hill in Grainger County. It did not seem much like a war to be wading in mud, sleet, rain, and snow without being able to engage the Federal forces. We were only exposing our troops to more misery and greater hardship although it was the general feeling that the war was winding down. We had been severely beaten, and our morale had plummeted. So with a break in the fighting, we took the opportunity to try and heal ourselves. However, just a short time later, I received some devastating news.

1865

In early January, I received word that my brother John was dead. His premonition had proven correct in the aftermath of his experience at Missionary Ridge. After we were separated, from what information I received later, John was on vidette duty between Dalton and Atlanta, Georgia, where his unit had been sent to help stop Major General Tecumseh Sherman's Federal forces from reaching Atlanta. Sherman had embarked on his famous "March to the Sea."

One night in late November or early December of last year, he was posted as vidette just outside the camp perimeter. Apparently, he had scouted too close to the Federal lines during his duty and was shot by one of their sharpshooters. John took a minié ball to the leg, which shattered his upper right thigh.

The minié ball was a new kind of ammunition shot from a different kind of musket that was first introduced during the War. Because of the musket's grooved barrel and matching special grooves on the minié ball, the minié ball spun much faster when it left the gun barrel. These rifled muskets were also far more accurate at a much longer range. The top of the minié ball, which was cone shaped, would flatten out when it hit something, usually a bone, resulting in a much more serious injury. Because of its shape and the fact that it was traveling faster, it would leave a gaping wound with a lot more damage to the bones and the soft tissue and muscles around the bones. This, in turn, led to more infection after the injury.

John did his best to crawl back to his own lines where he was then dragged to safety by his fellow soldiers who carried him on a stretcher to the nearest field hospital. From there, he was transported by horse-drawn ambulance to the regimental hospital. When his condition was stabilized, or so they thought, he was taken by special railroad car on the Western and Atlantic Railroad south from Dalton through Resaca, Allatoona, Big Shanty, and Kennesaw Station to Atlanta. From there, he was transported east on the Georgia Railroad to Blackie Hospital in Augusta, Georgia.

Because the wound did not heal properly due to the unsanitary conditions that existed and just the lack of general sanitation practices, his leg wound reopened, and he died from the ensuing fever and infection.

John did not want his leg amputated. This was the most common practice of fixing such wounds since bone splinters in the leg would virtually assure improper healing. John said he would take his chances with the leg recovering because "a farmer can't farm with one leg." He was a proud man to the end. John died at Blackie Hospital on Monday, December 5, 1864. Mourning was now a widow, and three young children were fatherless.

During our time in the army, John and I had covered a lot of ground in Kentucky, Tennessee, Virginia, and Georgia.

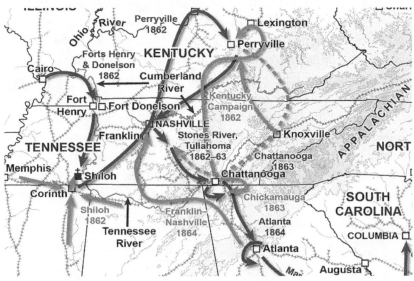

Map by Hal Jespersen, www.cwmaps.com, CC by 3.0,
https://commons.wikimedia.org/w/index.php?curid=17811342.

Upon hearing the news of my brother's death and the fact that we were close to the Bays Mountain area, I was granted a ten-day furlough to head home with the bad news. News like this generally traveled faster through the army ranks than by any dispatches sent from some headquarters somewhere. They were already dealing with a mountain of correspondence because of all the war casualties, and John was just one more.

As I traveled the lonely country roads on horseback to Bays Mountain, I tried to imagine in my mind the words I would have to say not only to John's widow, Mourning, but also to my mother and father. Now, John was gone, and I was the oldest son. I felt a heavy weight on my shoulders as the countryside slowly slipped by. Slowed by rain-swollen streams and creeks, along with the constant mud, it seemed like forever before I could see the familiar area around McPheeter's Bend near the Holston River. I knew it would not be long before I would be ascending Bays Mountain at Laurel Run.

I arrived at our home on Bays Mountain on Tuesday, January 10, 1865. I received what could only be modestly described as a very warm welcome from Amanda! We had not seen each other for over two years. Even though she was surprised to see me, she realized why I was there when I told her about John. Amanda was shocked and deeply saddened, for John had been a wonderful brother-in-law. But, as she normally does, she stopped thinking about herself almost immediately; and her words were of deep concern for my parents, sisters, Mourning, and her children. We sat down to discuss how to tell the rest of the family and decided it would be best to invite them all over for supper sometime toward the end of the week. With that decided, we had some catching up to do. For the first time in over two years, instead of sleeping in tents or out in the open with other men, horses, or mules, I slept in the loving arms of the woman I love.

The next two weeks went by quickly as we took care of seeing the rest of the family and telling them about John's death. It was a shock to us all, of course; but the picture that will remain in my mind is my parents and Mourning, along with her children, hugging each other in a group and crying together until it seemed like the tears would never end. I guess they never do and never will. John's death was a huge loss to the family and left a gaping hole of sadness and grief.

Amanda and I spent as much time as we could together, knowing that I would have to return to my company in a few days. When it came time to say goodbye, this time was more heart wrenching than the first time back in December 1862. Knowing what had now happened to John, Amanda had real concerns about the same thing happening to me. I tried to convince her that I was just a lowly teamster and blacksmith, but my words did little to comfort her. She knew that I was close enough to where the fighting was taking place to understand the danger I was in.

We prayed together on the front porch of our home and left my fate in the hands of the Lord. As I rode away down the narrow mountain trail, I turned for one last look to see Amanda standing there, her young, beautiful face stained with tears.

Rejoining my unit, we continued to skirmish off and on in eastern Tennessee during the spring of 1865. One cool, clear, crisp day in mid-March, a dozen other blacksmiths and I were ordered to go west to the bridge at Strawberry Plains. It was still in a state of disrepair after being destroyed last June. And so it was here that my life took a different turn, for the better.

Bridge over Strawberry Plains, ca 1860s, Library of Congress

On April 24, 1865, as I was working on part of the trestle, I was captured at gunpoint by Federal soldiers. They were exceedingly kind to me as they could clearly see that I posed no threat to them. I had no gun, and my blacksmith's hammer was well out of reach when they surprised me and the others as we were absorbed in our work. Sentries had not been posted because no Federal forces had been reported in the area for weeks.

I was captured exactly fifteen days after General Robert E. Lee surrendered the last major Confederate army to General Ulysses S. Grant at Appomattox Court House on April 9, 1865. News traveled slowly in those days; and the war continued for months afterward as, one by one, other Confederate commands were surrendered.

Following my capture at Strawberry Plains, we (I and several hundred others) were transported by railcar 127 miles to Chattanooga where I was "interviewed" and told that the war was over. I was given fresh clothing to replace my tattered Confederate uniform, and then we traveled another 134 miles to Nashville where I was told that it would be in my best interests to sign an oath of allegiance to the United States of America. I did not argue with them.

On April 29, 1865, exactly five days and 261 miles later, I pledged my allegiance to the country I had always loved. The country had changed, but my feelings for it were the same as before the war. My brother and I were just home-loving, simple people who felt compelled to fight a war to protect our homes while the politicians who were responsible for bringing our country to this point had made angry speeches from the pulpits of safe city streets about constitutional rights. Now, John was dead, and his widow and their three children would have to live without a devoted husband and father. A few months after learning of John's death, Mourning and her three children moved back to where her mother lived in her native Elm Creek District, Stones Chapel Community in Grayson County, Virginia.

Even with this sense of loss, a wave of relief swept over me that I could now return to my beloved Amanda. I would have signed any paper to make that happen. I just wanted to go home.

The general terms of the surrender of Confederate forces to Federal troops was enforced throughout the days that followed Lee's surrender to Grant at Appomattox Court House. Even though Lee surrendered the Army of Northern Virginia, there were still other regiments that continued to fight for weeks until seeing the futility of it. Grant understood that most men in the Southern ranks were small farmers. Therefore, he let all men who claimed to own a horse or mule take the animals home with them to work their farms. Grant knew that without the use of horses or mules, it was doubtful that we would be able to put in a crop to carry ourselves and our families through the next winter. Another condition was that we would be able to travel free on government transports and military railroads to reach our homes. Without saying it, many of us were incredibly grateful that General Grant was so kind in victory.

There were hundreds of us captured at Strawberry Plains, and we were told by our captors of the general conditions of surrender. I was lucky enough to catch a ride on a flatbed railcar that was so crowded we had to sit, or stand, shoulder to shoulder until the train had to stop due to blown-up and destroyed tracks. Then, it was every man for himself. Some walked, and some rode their horses or mules. I mostly walked through the open countryside, having to skirt impassable roads from time to time. The land was blackened and flattened here and there by the weapons of war, but knowing that each step brought me closer to Bays Mountain and our home put a renewed spring in my step.

I had a sweet arrival at home on May 16, 1865, when Amanda informed me that I was going to be a father as the result of my ten-day furlough last January. I was overwhelmed with happiness! I was back home with Amanda and starting a family! We still missed our little Elizabeth, but the thought of starting anew brought tremendous joy to us. Since we were going to have another mouth to feed, I figured I needed to make a quick change from wartime to peacetime. So, by June 7, I was well into planting the seeds of our crops that we hoped would flourish on our small plot of land on top of Bays Mountain. I was thrilled to know I was going to be a father, but little did I know that my future would also involve planting a church.

Post-Civil War, 1865–1902 Family, Farming, and Ministry

The war had destroyed large parts of our way of life in Tennessee. Although our area around Bays Mountain was mostly spared from the effects of the war, other places not too far away were greatly damaged by the battles, skirmishes, and occupation. There was widespread destruction of homes, outbuildings, wells, fences, crops, and livestock. Most of the menfolk were away during the war, so many farms fell into a state of neglect with overgrown fields and such. We were fortunate in that several young neighbor boys were able to help Amanda keep our farm running as best she could.

Upon returning home from the war, I found a cheerfulness and resilience with which the people were working to restore their former condition. Tennessee was the first southern state to be readmitted to the Union on July 24, 1866, and we hoped this would set an example for the rest of the Confederate states to follow suit and begin the long process of healing our great country.

People everywhere were anxious to put the war behind them and get back to the task of farming and taking care of our families. Amanda and I, together with my parents and siblings still at home, began the difficult and arduous task of rebuilding our farms. We also began what was to become a large family, starting with the birth of John James on October 11, 1865.

When we began our family after the war, we were very blessed to have Mrs. Grace Epley in our lives. She lived just down the road about a quarter of a mile, then back up the trail to the left, and on the other side of the ridge. Mrs. Epley was a midwife; and through her efforts, we were able to bring eight new babies into the world, all of whom survived. Every one of them was greatly anticipated and welcomed into our ever-growing family.

Nearly all the births at this time took place in the home with most families averaging six children. On Bays Mountain, Mrs. Epley was responsible for many of the births. She was very skilled in assisting Amanda by providing her with comfort, food, and a nurturing manner and patiently waiting for nature to take its course. She was also very patient with me, the worrying father, as the process evolved.

Mrs. Epley always seemed old to me, but perhaps it was her premature silver-gray hair that created this impression. She was a petite woman but strong and sinewy with small hands. Having been a hardworking farm girl all her life, her hands had held the reins of a mule and the handles of a plow, so they were not going to be denied the birth of any child. Mrs. Epley's determination during the births of all eight of our children was evident and resolute. Each time, for her efforts, she gladly accepted payment in the form of a fried chicken, a smoked ham, or a package of side pork. Bartering was a way of life, and we were thankful that Mrs. Epley was a part of that. The name Grace was given to her for a reason.

As the years rolled by, our family grew and grew. Nancy, our second daughter, came along November 10, 1867. William arrived December 14, 1869. Christian joined us February 25, 1872. Our daughters, Susanna, born March 15, 1874, and Martha, born May 2, 1876, continued to bless our family. Mary Jane arrived July 1, 1879, and to top off the family, Matilda was born February 13, 1883.

The hard work needed to keep a farm and family running required a rock-solid faith. The Lord guided us and gave us strength on all those days when the work seemed overwhelming. We *believed in* the Trinity of the Father, Son, and Holy Spirit. We also *lived by* the trilogy of faith, family, and food.

My family always had plenty of mouthwatering mountain-cooking food recipes. Rabbits, squirrels, and other game were plentiful on Bays Mountain. Hunting was a favorite pastime for the boys as they were growing up in the Tennessee woods. During the day, the boys—John, William, and Christian—hunted deer, wild turkeys, rabbits, partridges, and squirrels which were abundant and helped to supply our table with wild game. At night, treeing raccoons with Walter, the family dog, in the lead proved to be a lot of fun. With our home-grown hogs, cattle, and chickens, we generally had plenty of meat for our meals.

One of my favorite simple recipes was rabbit crust pot pie. I would take a nice rabbit, freshly shot and skinned by one of the boys, cut it up, and let stand in saltwater for a while. Then, I would put it on to boil. While I was doing this, Amanda would cut two onions into very fine pieces and season with pepper, salt, and butter; this was stewed until tender and thickened with brown gravy. Amanda always made plenty of thick brown gravy because you had to have enough to cover the crust.

For the brown gravy, we would take a teacupful of flour, put it in a hot skillet, and stir until every particle of flour was nicely browned and well done. Then, we mixed in cold water thoroughly and stirred in the rabbit until it was a nice thick gravy.

For the baked crust, we put a half pint of flour in a bread bowl with a little salt, a teaspoonful of baking powder, and a small spoonful of lard rubbed through the flour, which is wet with cream, and mixed lightly and soft. This was then rolled out half an inch thick and baked in a large turkey pan. We would spread it all over, take a knife, and cut the dough in long strips. When it was baked nice and brown, we broke it in pieces, put it in a dish, and covered with the gravy.

Other favorite recipes included the following from handwritten recipe cards or notes passed down from prior members of the family:

Rabbit Stew

Cut up a full-grown young rabbit, soak a few minutes in water, and put into a vessel with water enough to almost cover. Let it boil until nearly done. Brown some flour in a skillet having in it some lard and a small onion finely sliced, and when the flour is brown enough, pour on some of the stock. Add all to the rabbit and season with salt, pepper, and vinegar. Let simmer from five to ten minutes.

Fried Squirrel

Take young squirrels about two-thirds grown, skin them and wash carefully, wipe dry, and lay on a beefsteak board. With a hammer, pound the meat until the bones are crushed and the meat tender. Salt the meat, roll in flour, and lay in a large frying pan containing hot butter or butter and lard mixed. Brown and turn. Watch closely, and soon they will be a golden brown and ready for the table in thirty minutes or less.

Squirrel Pie

Carefully skin and clean a pair of squirrels, cut in pieces, put in a stew pan, and cook with two slices of salt pork with enough water to stew them about half done. Season and thicken the gravy. Put into a deep dish, cover with a nice thick pie crust, and bake in a moderate oven until done.

How to Cook a 'Possum (Old-Time Plantation Style)

This was always one of my favorite recipes. You could either shoot or trap a possum, but whichever method was used, a good possum is a dead possum. If you happened to livetrap one, lay the possum on the ground and put a stick across his neck. Then, put a foot on each end of the stick and pull his tail until his neck pops.

Boil a kettle of hot water and throw in a couple of shovels of ashes to make the hair slip; then throw him in the boiling water. Wait a while and then take the hair off and scrape the possum with a butcher knife until he is as white as paper. Next, split him open, take his insides out, and wash clean with cold water. You will need to peel and slice some potatoes (sweet potatoes are better if you have them); put the slices in the possum and sew him up.

Put the sewed-up carcass in a kettle of hot water and keep slowly boiling until tender, which could take about two hours. Possums are tough little critters! Take the possum from the kettle and place in a bake pan and, at the same time, add additional boiled potatoes and place around him in the pan. Set the pan in a hot stove ready for baking with butter, salt, and black pepper all over. Then, brown nicely.

Our family was very resourceful in that we were able to use what the land naturally provided and add that to what we were able to produce ourselves.

My family and I always had a strong bond with the soil. We loved the land and everything in it. Farming had always been our way of life. It is a simple life of providing for ourselves and helping our neighbors when needed and not being afraid to ask them for help. Over the years, we helped each other build our log homes and clear the land. Our farm, tucked into the countryside on Bays Mountain, was like heaven to me. It did not matter what season it was; there was a God-given beauty about each one of them.

I was thankful that my best friends, Porter and William, made it back to Hawkins County when the war ended. They were in Northwest Georgia at the time and had been serving with John until he was killed. Both had ridden mules back home. It was great to see them, and we spent a great deal of time together catching up on old times. We helped each other over the months and years to establish our farms. The two of them had eventually bought farms of their own and began raising families after each had gotten married to a couple of local beauties. Porter had purchased a farm near McPheeter's Bend, and William was a little further east and south of the Holston River.

Many years later, I also found out that our drummer boy, Johnny "Cadence" McKinney, had made it back to Grainger County, gotten married, and started a family and a farm. Same was true with Dustin "Dusty" Odom. He got back to Greene County in one piece, gotten married and started a farm and family. All of us had really bonded during the war, and it was good to know that all had made it back and were getting on with life.

My ministry had evolved over time since the days of my youth. My father and mother had embraced the Dunkard Brethren faith early in their married life. Not only was my family of English descent but also a fair sprinkling of German along the way. The name Dunkard or Dunker is derived from the Pennsylvania German word for *dunke*, which comes from the German word *tunken*, meaning "to dunk" or "to dip." This emphasizes the method of baptism observed by our branch of the Brethren for "thrice" or "trine" immersion. A believer is immersed three times: once in the name of the Father, once in the name of the Son, and once in the name of the Holy Spirit, all with a forward motion.

My faith had grown during the war, and my survival made me realize that God had a plan for my life. After the war, I could feel a gentle tugging at my soul to begin meeting with my neighbors on a regular basis to study the Word of God. With the grace of God, I believed we might someday be able to establish a church. In the meantime, we could meet in homes or outside when the weather was nice. A great place to meet outside was next to the Bowser Cemetery, which was established in 1840. Little did I know, but God already had that in His plans.

I never attended college or seminary and was never ordained. In my day, anyone who had a good working knowledge of the Word could be a lay preacher or village minister, as we were often called, at most churches. For as long as I can remember, I have had a deep love and reverence for our Lord and Savior, Jesus Christ. My mother can be credited with instilling in me a strong and abiding faith in God.

She would say, "When the truth of the Word is not being taught, we will do things that are contrary to God's Holiness." Then, she would continue, "Our hearts can only be eternally filled by a God that comes from eternity. We should be asking ourselves this question every day, What can I do for God today?" My mother had an immense amount of wisdom, and I concluded that she was right.

This abiding faith and love had served me well throughout my early adulthood and, especially, during my time in the Civil War.

I was always blessed with a clear, strong voice. Amanda jokingly told me that it was acquired through calling in the hogs at night or calling in the children for dinner. She claimed that during most sermons, my voice sounded like thunder and could vibrate the sides of Bays Mountain.

I loved to hear good stories and could tell a pretty good one myself. I believe these traits endeared me to my family, friends, neighbors, and, later, to my congregation at Dunkard Church. My easygoing conversational style enhanced my sermons. But I was not without a little hellfire as well, and oftentimes my passion for the Lord took over.

In my sermons, I liked to use common, everyday situations and events in combination with scripture to get my message across. I liked to talk about Jesus as if I were talking about my best friend. I was filled with wonder when I tried to describe what heaven would be like. Describing hell filled me with loathing and an urgency for people to accept the Lord Jesus Christ as their personal Savior. This was particularly important for young people who had not yet made that decision. I spoke of Calvary with a love and gentleness that only a suffering Jesus could bring to the world.

When we were meeting in people's homes, I would jump on the family mule, Jingles Jr. (Jingles had passed on by this time), and ride to the home. Amanda and the children would join me, and we would take turns riding and walking. The kids would squeal with joy as I

lifted them up high and placed them on the back of the mule. I could get at least three of the little ones on his back at one time and a couple of the older ones.

I was able to baptize many people, old and young, over the years.

These baptisms took place at a quiet spot in the pool of water at the base of Laurel Run Falls. The falls and the pool were a perfect setting just down the mountainside from what was to be the future site of our church. There is a winding trail through the woods to the falls. Rocks and fallen trees provided the seating for the congregation as they witnessed the holy event. It is the perfect place for the new believer to proclaim their faith in the Creator.

In addition to baptisms and weddings, I was also called upon to perform funerals as well. The most difficult funeral at which I spoke was my father's. He passed away quietly at his home on Bays Mountain on Friday, November 13, 1874, at the age of sixty-three.

I was hesitant at first to perform my father's funeral knowing that my emotions would come to the surface no matter how hard I tried to keep them in check. What helped me decide was knowing he had been a man of God for practically all his life, and what better way to honor my father and our Heavenly Father than by speaking of my love for both of them. In the end, I performed his funeral service on Sunday, November 15, underneath of his favorite oak tree in his backyard. Most of the congregation were there to pay their respects on what was a beautiful autumn day. The oak tree and the surrounding countryside were in full late-autumn splendor as if the limbs and leaves were quietly singing out praise for the Creator of the universe.

Following the service, I led the procession with his pinewood casket the short distance to the Bowser Cemetery where we laid him to rest just a few steps from what was to become the site of our new church.

Little did I know it at the time; but the man who married Amanda and me, Jacob Hamilton, had a plan in mind for this special site on top of Bays Mountain. When Jacob sprung the news on me about the new church, I was thrilled and could not wait to formally dedicate the site for which I prepared the following speech.

Dedication of Dunkard Church Site
Saturday, September 29, 1877

Good evening and welcome to all our family, friends, and neighbors here in Hawkins County. In the crowd, I see not only members of my own family but other folks from the Arnold, Barrett, Bowser, Cavin, Crawford, and Goad families, among others. Again, welcome to all of you. For years now, we have been meeting in the homes of our congregation, and what a blessing that has been. But now is the time the Lord has provided to grow His Family. We have an opportunity to dedicate this spot for a new church. Before we do that, I would like to read scripture from the New Testament regarding the building of His Church. Then, we will begin with a word of prayer.

First, from Matthew 16:18, the Bible says, "And I say also unto thee, That thou art Peter, and upon this rock I will build my church; and the gates of hell shall not prevail against it." The New Testament church was a local congregation or assembly of believers, which is a church in and of itself. This verse is the first time the word *church* is used in the New Testament.

Second, from 1 Corinthians 3:11, we read, "For other foundation can no man lay than that is laid, which is Jesus Christ." This is a reminder to us that the foundation is always the least noticed but the most important part of any building. The Apostle Paul laid the foundation of the first church, and we are urged to think about not only *what* we build but *how* we build. The very nature of the foundation is Jesus Christ.

Finally, in Hebrews 3:4, we read, "For every house is built by some man; but he that built all things is God." Therefore, we know that Jesus Christ, the Builder, is God.

Let us pray.

Heavenly Father, we give you thanks for this time that we can share together to dedicate this piece of land for a church and school to honor your Holy Name. We are grateful to the Hamilton family who so graciously gave the deed to this land just this morning. Thank you for the beautiful evening here on the mountaintop in which to hold this service.

Lord, we pray that you will guide us in not only the building of this church and school but that, when built, you will give us the wisdom to grow it to include more of your children and that we can educate our young ones to grow to be a blessing to you.

Help us, Lord, to teach all the doctrines of Your Son, Jesus Christ. Let us yearn for peace, love, unity, and both faith and works. Guide us as a people who, as little children, accept Your Word as a message from heaven.

Again, Lord, we give you the honor and the glory in Jesus' Holy Name. Amen.

At this time, I would like to read to you the entire land conveyance so that all of you can hear the very words written by our brother, Jacob Hamilton. The conveyance reads as follows:

Know all now by these present. That for the love and interest that I, Jacob Hamilton, have and entertain for the education of the children of the community and for the preaching of the Gospels for the good of society, I do hereby give, transfer, and convey to Jessee Simpson, William Crawford and G. B. Gilbert as trustees & their successors forever, a certain piece or parcel of land containing one acre more or less situated in the 5th District of Hawkins County, Tennessee for the purpose of building a Church & School house thereon. Which land is known and bounded as follows to wit; Beginning at the branch near a large chestnut where Gilbert's line crosses said branch then N.E. poles to a stake are B. Hamilton's lines then with his lines N.W. poles to a stake thence S.W. poles to a stake in Gilbert's lines then with his lines S.E. poles to the beginning. Together with all the appurtenances and interest that I have in and to said land. And I covenant with the said trustees to warrant and defend the title to said piece of land to said trustees & their successors against the claim of all persons claiming by or through are given.

Attest: Under my hand & said Sept. 29th 1877
J. Hamilton
(Seal)

That will conclude our dedication service this evening. We look forward to the building of His church and school. I have been told that we have plenty of strong able-bodied men to begin this work. With the Lord's blessing, we should be able to have our first sermon in the new church by early next year.

Let us close with several final passages from scripture and a word of prayer.

Ephesians 2:19–22 says:

"Now therefore ye are no more strangers and foreigners, but fellow citizens with the saints, and of the household of God; And are built upon the foundation of the apostles and the prophets, Jesus Christ himself being the chief cornerstone;

In whom all the building fitly framed together groweth unto an holy temple in the Lord: In whom ye also are built together for an habitation of God through the Spirit."

Heavenly Father, we thank you again for your blessings on this congregation, and we look forward to the building of Your Church. Be with each of us as we think about what part we can do to make this church and school a reality. We give you all the honor and praise in Jesus' name. Amen.

We all pulled together to build the Dunkard Church on Bays Mountain over a three-and-a-half-month period, October through December 1877. The tiny church was built alongside of Bowser Cemetery, which was established in 1840. The foundation and cornerstones were solid rock, mostly limestone, which is native to the area. Together, Jessee Simpson, William Crawford, Mr. Hamilton, and I each took a turn placing a symbolic cornerstone to outline the area of the new church.

The church was made of sturdy large rough-hewn logs with a couple of shorter similar-type logs as the front steps for the door, which faced east. Because site selection is the most important aspect of building, the site alongside of Bowser Cemetery was perfect. This site provided us with both ample sunlight and drainage. The church was built without the use of nails and derived its stability from simple stacking of the logs. Careful notching reduced the size of the gap between logs which were then chinked together with a combination of small stones and mud. Only a few dowel joints here and there were needed for reinforcement. This is because a log building tends to compress slightly as it settles over a few months or years. Nails would soon be out of alignment and torn out.

As the church progressed during the rather mild winter of 1877, it was with great joy that we watched each hewed log be lifted into place. We planned four windows on the north side and four windows on the south side. The church was built with a moderate pitch to the roof and topped off with cedar shake shingles.

The interior of the church was furnished with split-log benches made from the abundant supply of nearby ash trees. A narrow strip of wood was attached to the back of the benches, just wide enough to lean against but not wide enough for someone to get too comfortable lest they fall asleep during one of my dynamic sermons. The inside was lit by a few coal oil lamps and heated by a tiny potbellied stove, vented with a metal chimney and located in the northwest corner. On cold Sundays, to stay warm, everyone tried to sit in this corner. At least it got the congregation to sit toward the front!

We lived close enough to the little church that I could walk to the services. In addition, it was a great place to meet with members of the congregation and the other two trustees to discuss the growth of the school, which was also held in the church. We discussed at length exactly what kind of school we should have for our children.

Obviously, the teaching and instruction had to be firmly rooted in God's Word. We believed that the Bible, coupled with a good education in the basics of reading, writing, and arithmetic, would be the greatest gift to our young people. Also, discipline, self-control, and the elevation of morals were key elements for the growth of our children. Education and discipline go hand in hand. Books for the school were purchased from the Brethren Publishing House located in Dayton, Ohio. I continued to utilize them for religious and devotional books until early 1901.

Out of our congregational discussions, we developed a *mission statement* for our school. After much discussion, we settled on the following:

1) Observe and obey God's commands.
2) Hold ourselves to high moral standards and remember our Creator.
3) Study faithfully.
4) Be gentle men and women in all things.
5) Keep the peace.

In addition to a rigorous course of school instruction, during most of the year when the weather was nice, the children were outside playing games such as leapfrog, marbles, roll the hoop, hopscotch, and hide-and-seek. During cold winter months, checkers and peg games were the favorites, along with various card games. Betting on any game was a mortal sin and was met instantly with a swift rebuke. We also encouraged each of the children to carve out a little time on a regular basis to read.

As the church was being built during the winter of 1877, I spent considerable time thinking about what my first sermon within its walls should be. It had to be special and uplifting for all of those who had labored so hard to build it and to Our Lord that we might give Him the praise and glory. I decided to preach on a favorite Psalm of mine—one that covers a lot of ground and the one that Amanda read before my baptism so many years ago.

My First Sermon at Dunkard Church
Sunday, January 13, 1878

Good morning, Congregation! Welcome to our new church. So glad to see all of you this beautiful, bright winter morning. We are so blessed to be here this morning to worship our Lord in our new church. To all of you who helped to build this house of worship, a sincere thank you and God bless you! Everyone has been working very hard since we dedicated this site last September.

Let us begin and set our hearts on God's Word by reading King David's prayer from 1 Chronicles, chapter 29, verses 10–13. God said that King David was a man after his own heart. Since this prayer came from King David's heart, it will be good for us to repeat. Please bow your heads and pray with me.

"Wherefore David blessed the Lord before all the congregation: and David said, "Blessed be thou, Lord God of Israel our Father, for ever and ever.

Thine, O Lord, is the greatness and the power, and the glory, and the victory, and the majesty: for all that is in the heaven and in the earth is thine; thine is the kingdom, O Lord, and thou art exalted as head above all.

Both riches and honour come of thee, and thou reignest over all; and in thine hand is power and might; and in thine hand it is to make great, and to give strength unto all.

Now therefore, our God, we thank thee, and praise thy glorious name."

Amen.

It is so warm and comforting to be in our new place of worship. This congregation, after meeting in homes for all these years, is so blessed as we start a new year. And we are reminded that all blessings come from and through our Lord and Savior, Jesus Christ. I think it would be fitting for our message this morning to be about what I consider to be one of the most beautiful of the Psalms, Psalm 103. This Psalm has been described as too much for a thousand pens to write. What a tribute to King David! It is apparent that he truly did pour out his heart to the Lord. This Psalm is such a delightful note of praise for the mercies of the Lord. It contains twenty-two verses, the exact number of letters in the Hebrew alphabet, and it ends with the exact words with which it began, "Bless the Lord, O my soul!" Let us begin by reading the first five verses together.

> "Bless the Lord, O my soul: and all
> that is within me, bless his holy
> name.
> Bless the Lord, O my soul, and forget
> not all his benefits:
> Who forgiveth all thine iniquities;
> who healeth all thy diseases;
> Who redeemeth thy life from destruc-
> tion; who crowneth thee with
> lovingkindness and tender
> mercies;
> Who satisfieth thy mouth with good
> things; so that thy youth is
> renewed like the eagle's."

To begin with, King David calls upon his soul, his immortal soul, which he says is all that is within him, all his senses and his very being, to bless the holy name of God. David has stirred up his innermost self so that he might magnify the Lord, and by so doing, it is with complete and total gratitude. When we are about to worship God, it would be shameful to offer him anything less than the utmost our souls can give. Look at the scripture and see that David calls for ALL that is within him to remember ALL the Lord's benefits. God's all cannot be praised with less than our all.

David, by writing this Psalm, is ready to count his many blessings and to name them one by one. How many times do each of us really sit down and count our blessings? Sometimes we say that in talking to others, "Don't forget to count your blessings." But do we? David, here, is prepared to do just that.

He begins his list of blessings by saying that he praises the God who forgives all his sins. THAT, my friends, is the greatest benefit we can receive from God! It is not only the continual forgiving of sins, but also he says he will heal all my diseases. No disease of our soul is too great for His healing power, and He will do so until the last stain is gone from our nature.

Going on with his list, David says he will not forget that God is the one who redeems his life from destruction, or from the pit of hell. He did this by purchasing through THE BLOOD OF JESUS CHRIST and by the power of HIS MIGHTY HAND! Redemption is one of the sweetest notes in the chorus of the redeemed.

David closes out these first five verses by saying that regardless of our age, we can find joy and happiness in blessing the name of the Lord and proclaiming all His benefits to us so that the strength of our youth is renewed. How wonderful is that! As I age, I yearn for the strength of my youth and praise the Lord for the life he has given me. Just think! We have the strength to soar over the problems that face us every day because we have a heart satisfied with God. The next two verses read as follows:

> "The Lord executeth righteousness and judgment for all that are oppressed.
> He made known his ways unto Moses, his acts unto the children of Israel."

Scripture is full of wisdom regarding the care of the oppressed. A civil war was fought not that many years ago, as most of you will remember, over the oppression of our fellow human beings. I believe that we, who wore the gray, were on the wrong side of our fellow man. We can only pray for forgiveness. Indeed, the Israelites cried out to the Lord for freedom from their oppressors. AND HE HEARD THEM! The Lord is the Creator of the human soul that yearns for freedom, and no man should ever be the slave of another. The Lord revealed Himself to Moses and the people of Israel as He led them throughout their wilderness journey from their enslavement in Egypt. We, as believers in Jesus, know the Lord's ways of grace, and we have been made to see His acts of mercy toward us. We must give our whole heart in praise to the Holy Spirit who has made these things known to us. For had it not been for Him, we would have continued in darkness until this day.

Our reading continues:

> "The Lord is merciful and gracious,
>   slow to anger, and plenteous in
>   mercy.
> He will not always chide; neither will
>   he keep his anger forever.
> He hath not dealt with us after our
>   sins; nor rewarded us according
>   to our iniquities."

In these three verses, David gives his full measure to praising God for His divine character. How wonderful it is to have a merciful and gracious Lord! God does not always punish us for our sin. He is slow to anger, bears no grudges, and harbors no resentments. Because of this, we should also learn to be slow to anger. If the Lord has that much patience with us, should we not endure the errors of our own Brethren? One of the most praiseworthy things about God is that He has not dealt with us as our sins deserve. If He did, we would all be sent to the lowest hell. We need to praise the Lord for what HE HAS NOT DONE to us, as well as for what HE HAS DONE for us. HE—IS—GOD, and He will accept repentance and atonement.

To understand the length and breadth of our Lord, verses eleven through thirteen give us a picture of His splendor. But His greatness is also bounded by His pity for us as humans and His matchless mercy.

"For as the heaven is high above
the earth, so great is his mercy
toward them that fear him.
As far as the east is from the west, so
far hath he removed our trans-
gressions from us.
Like as a father pitieth his children, so
the Lord pitieth them that fear
him."

Sin can only be removed by the miracle of
God's love and Christ's atonement. His mercy is
the cause and the degree of forgiveness for us. The
reason for this mercy is clear—as we have mercy
and compassion on our children, so the Lord has
mercy and compassion on those who fear Him.
Like the respect a child has for his earthly father,
so it is done when we show that same godly fear
toward our Heavenly Father. Then, His great
mercy is given to us. The next three verses show
us how we, as humans, measure up, and they give
a good example of man's frailty. Please read along
with me:

"For He knoweth our frame; He
remembereth that we are dust.
As for man, his days are as grass:
as a flower of the field, so he
flourisheth.
For the wind passeth over it, and it is
gone; and the place thereof shall
know it no more."

God knows that we are fragile, feeble, and,
when left to ourselves, we are utterly helpless.
WE—NEED—GOD! We are pictured in the Psalm

as a flower of the field that flourishes and blooms brightly, but our lives are short lived. Then, the wind passes over us, and we are gone. Compare our short-lived lives to the everlasting person of God. God does not change. As He was in the beginning, He will be forever!

> "But the mercy of the Lord is from ever-
>   lasting to everlasting upon them
>   that fear him, and his righteous-
>   ness unto children's children;
> To such as keep his covenant, and to
>   those that remember his com-
>   mandments to do them."

Here, in these two verses, King David talks about the brief character of man's life with the everlasting character of God's mercy. God's divine mercy is FROM EVERLASTING, meaning that from eternity past, the Lord has seen His own children through the eyes of mercy. David continues that divine mercy is TO EVERLASTING! What a glorious thought! As it is with God, his mercy does not change. But God's mercy cannot be claimed until it is claimed by His grace. We do not know God's mercy until we know it in His Son, Jesus Christ.

The next verse, verse nineteen, stands alone in its glory as David prepares us for his final praise to God.

> "The Lord hath prepared his throne
>   in the heavens; and his kingdom
>   ruleth over all."

See the picture that this verse shows of the power and majesty of God as He sits on His throne established in the heavens. He rules over all the kingdoms of the world, a promise that will find its final fulfillment when the kingdoms of this world become the kingdoms of our Lord and of His Christ, AND HE SHALL REIGN FOREVER AND EVER!

We conclude Psalm 103 with the final three verses. As we read them, you will see that they form a final triad of verses to form a trilogy of praise to God. Let us read them together:

> "Bless the Lord, ye his angels: that excel in strength, that do his commandments, hearkening unto the voice of his word.
> Bless ye the Lord, all ye his hosts; ye ministers of his, that do his pleasure.
> Bless the Lord, all his works in all places of his dominion: bless the Lord, O my soul."

All of God's creation is called to bless the Lord beginning with the angels, the highest and most glorious beings that surround the throne of God. His heavenly hosts and ministers who do His will are called to bless the Lord, and finally, all His works everywhere in the universe He created are called to bless His Holy Name. And all God's children shout AMEN!

I did many, many sermons in our church, practically every Sunday over the years. I was blessed with a faithful ever-growing congregation who encouraged me, prayed with me, and prayed for me. The years continued to roll by, and our time was spent farming, raising our children, and being pastor to the congregation as we all worked together to live our lives according to God's plan.

My mother passed away on Thursday, May 27, 1886. Unlike my father's funeral many years before, my mother's funeral was held in the church on Sunday, May 30, 1886, on a glorious spring day. I, once again, felt the need to perform the service knowing full well that it was going to be every bit as difficult as my father's.

My mother was the person who developed my faith early in my life. She was the essence of a saint who openly practiced the fruit of the Spirit to all she came in contact: love, joy, peace, patience, kindness, goodness, faithfulness, gentleness, and self-control. She imparted as much wisdom as she could to me, and I am forever grateful to her for that. We buried her alongside my father in the Bowser Cemetery, and after the service was over, I lingered near their graves and observed the many other family and friends that we had laid to rest in this peaceful spot on top of our beloved Bays Mountain.

Prior to my mother's passing, our two oldest children, John and Nancy, grew to adulthood and found spouses with whom to share their lives. John and his wife stayed pretty close to the homeplace and began lives of their own. About a year and a half after Mom's funeral, it was William's time to fly from the nest. And in what seemed like the shortest period of my life, between 1890 and 1901, the remainder of our brood—Christian, Susanna, Martha, Mary Jane, and Matilda—grew up and left our home to begin lives of their own. Five of our children—Nancy, William, Christian, Susanna, and Mary Jane—upon their marriages, migrated to the black, fertile soil of southeast and southwest Iowa, where they raised their families in and around Keokuk and Hamburg. With this many children, we were blessed with a large number of grandchildren. At times, it seemed we had more than you could shake a stick at!

My health began to fail in early 1901. I was still as actively involved in farming and ministry to the extent that my energy level allowed me. But I also had a feeling that my time was getting short, and I began to prepare for my passing. Most of my family had lived well past the normal life span for this time, and I was fast approaching the age at which my father died. As the year went along, I got weaker and weaker from what most would say was "just old age." There were a few things I needed to bring to a conclusion, and the one at the top of the list was giving up my preaching at the church. I had been doing this now for over twenty-three years. Preparing my sermons for each Sunday service was taking a tremendous toll on me. I decided to relinquish my duties at the church in August and began to prepare my final sermon.

My Final Sermon at Dunkard Church
Sunday, August 25, 1901

Good morning, Congregation! And thank you for all your prayers in recent weeks. Most of you know that I am ill and the strength in my body is slowly failing. I want to formally say that this will be my last sermon to you.

As I look out upon you, my heart is warmed by the love and friendship that you have given to me and Amanda over these many years as your pastor. My first sermon in this church was January 13, 1878, over twenty-three years ago. In that time, many of us have raised our children and have seen them leave the nest.

Please permit me to reminisce a little bit. Some of us have known each other since we were in our late teens. We have been witnesses to many events in our lives such as the birth of our children and the death of our parents. Some of us served in the Civil War together, and some, like my brother John, never made it back home. It seems like an eternity ago, but it was just yesterday, wasn't it? I see some of you nodding your heads. Time passes and waits for no one. Each day brings us limited time, and only the Good Lord knows how much time each of us has.

That is why we need to be ready when He calls us home to be with Him. For reasons that we will never know or understand, the Lord called home our first child, Elizabeth, when she was but twenty days old. That was back in September 1862. Since then, Amanda and I were blessed with eight more children. I see Amanda is looking at me as if to say, "It's no wonder I'm worn out!" To you, Amanda, I will simply say thank you for a beautiful family and a wonderful life together of nearly forty-one years. You are the love of my life, and I thank God that He brought you into my life all those years ago. This new century promises to be an exciting one.

My prayer this morning is this:

Heavenly Father, we thank you for blessing us not only as individual families but also as Your church family. We thank you for Your love and mercy on each of us. Be with us as we go through the days and months ahead. You are our strength for each day, and we believe your promise of eternal life when we pass on. In Jesus' name, we pray. Amen.

We will have several readings this morning starting in the book of John 11:25,26. Jesus is talking to Martha, the sister of Lazarus, just before He raised Lazarus from the dead.

> "Jesus said unto her, I am the resurrection and the life: he that believeth in me, though he were dead, yet shall he live;
>
> And whosoever liveth and believeth in me shall never die."

We continue reading in 2 Corinthians 5:1:

"For we know that if our earthly
house of this tabernacle were dis-
solved, we have a building of God, a
house not made with hands, but eternal in the heavens."

This is God's promise! Eternal life is just
that—ETERNAL LIFE!
For it says in 1 John 5:11–13:

"And this is the record, that God
hath given to us eternal life, and this
life is in His Son.
He that hath the Son hath life;
and he that hath not the Son of God
hath not life.
These things have I written unto
you that believe on the name of the Son
of God; that ye may know that ye have
eternal life, and that ye may believe on
the name of the Son of God."

Brethren, death is not the end of life. It is
the gateway to eternity with God. The Bible is
God's blueprint for life and life everlasting. Those
who are born again can never be unborn. We are
born again in Christ, and we shall live with Him
forever.
The final reading for today is one which all
of you have probably read dozens of times. It is a
Psalm that we read or think about when we seek
His peace, love, and mercy. Some of us have written it on a scrap of paper and always carry it with
us. Others have memorized it. It is probably the

most famous of all the Psalms. Let me read Psalm 23 to you one last time as your pastor.

> "The Lord is my Shepherd; I shall not want.
> He maketh me to lie down in green pastures: he leadeth me beside the still waters.
> He restoreth my soul: he leadeth me in the paths of righteousness for his name's sake.
> Yea, though I walk through the valley of the shadow of death, I will fear no evil: for thou art with me; thy rod and thy staff they comfort me.
> Thou preparest a table before me in the presence of mine enemies: thou anointest my head with oil; my cup runneth over.
> Surely goodness and mercy shall follow me all the days of my life: and I will dwell in the house of the Lord forever."

Brothers and sisters in Christ, my health is failing me, but I do not fear the shadow of death. Because the Lord Jesus Christ has taken away the sting of death, the shadow of death cannot destroy my faith.

When we come to know God personally through His Son, Jesus Christ, the wall of death is shattered. All who have trusted in Christ as Savior have freedom from the fear of death. And so I can only ask what is written in Psalm 116:12–15:

"What shall I render unto the Lord for all his benefits toward me? I will take the cup of salvation and call upon the name of the Lord. I will pay my vows unto the Lord now in the presence of all His people. Precious in the sight of the Lord is the death of his saints."

The last sentence in that passage might sound a little strange to some of you, but the Lord treasures the death of his people. For in our passing, He welcomes us home with Him.

As a child of God who has walked in the path of the Good Shepherd, I am always at home with God. As it is written about heaven, Revelation 21:4 says, "And God shall wipe away all tears from their eyes; and there shall be no more death, neither sorrow, nor crying, neither shall there be any more pain: for the former things are passed away." And the Shepherd has also promised me: "I will never leave thee, nor forsake thee, I will be with thee always, even until the end of the ages."

Whether through the green pastures of Bays Mountain, the still waters of Laurel Run Creek, in the presence of my enemies, or through the valley of the shadow of death, I know He is always with me. Praise the Lord; and God bless you all, my family, friends, and neighbors. Thank you for being a part of our story.

I had one final deed that I needed to tend to and that was regarding Amanda. We'd shared a wonderful life together full of love, hard work, children, and all that goes with ministering to the needs of our church congregation. I decided to write one final letter to her but not tell her about it because I knew she would find it anyway. It would be something she could hold on to in remembrance of me.

My Final Love Letter to Amanda
Thursday, July 24, 1902

Dearest beloved Amanda,

I have not needed to write you a letter since shortly before the end of the war, over thirty-seven years ago. By the grace of God, we have been together nearly every day since then.

I am writing this letter to you because I feel my death is just weeks away now, and I wanted just one last time to tell you how much you mean to me. I can tell you face to face, but this letter can be kept by you and reread often after I am gone. I am placing it in my Bible, and I trust the Lord that you will find it tucked inside the pages of 1 Corinthians 13, our favorite Bible chapter as husband and wife. We have read it to each other many times over the years, and I hope it brings back many memories.

You have been my love, my life, and the primary foundation of my emotional strength since the day we met over forty-two years ago. I remember it as if it were yesterday, July 4, 1860. We were so young and full of life. My love for you has grown every day since that beautiful day at Laurel Run.

Our life together on Bays Mountain has had its share of struggles, but I count each day a blessing as your husband. If not for the war, we would have been together nearly every day, working our farm, raising our wonderful children, building a church and school, and being surrounded by special families as neighbors.

Amanda, we have truly been blessed. Our children are our legacy. They will long outlive us. And I hope they visit us often when, one day, we will rest beside each other at the Bowser Cemetery; and perhaps they can sit quietly in the church there and be with our God as they remember us in their thoughts and prayers.

As the Bible says in Psalm 103:15–17,

> "As for man, his days are as grass; as a flower of the field, so he flourisheth. For the wind passeth over it, and it is gone; and the place thereof shall know it no more. But the mercy of the Lord is from everlasting to everlasting upon them that fear Him, and his righteousness unto children's children."

Please share this passage with our children and grandchildren so that they might understand we all need the mercy and grace that only our Lord and Savior, Jesus Christ, can offer.

My hand is growing unsteady as I try and finish this letter to you. It has drained me of my strength, but my total and absolute love for you shall never waver as long as I can draw a breath.

I love you with all my heart, Amanda, and I look forward to sharing our life together in Eternity.

Forever yours,
Green

Afterword

After continuing in ill health for a few more weeks, Green Berry Gilbert died in the bounds of the Old Dunkard/Pleasant Mount Church and went to be with the Lord on Wednesday, August 13, 1902. Funeral services were conducted by G. W. Watson. Scripture reading was from 2 Timothy 4:6–8 which proclaims:

> "For I am now ready to be offered, and the time of my departure is at hand. I have fought a good fight, I have finished my course, I have kept the faith: Henceforth there is laid up for me a crown of righteousness, which the Lord, the righteous judge, shall give me at that day: and not to me only, but unto all them also that love his appearing."

He is buried alongside his father, Harvey Greenville Gilbert, and his mother, Nancy Fee Gilbert, in the Bowser Cemetery high on top of Bays Mountain, just a stone's throw from Laurel Run Falls. It is a beautiful spot for his final resting place.

Today, there is a new church, which was built at the Bowser Cemetery on the site of the original log church. It was renamed the Pleasant Mount Church.

Amanda filed for a widow's pension under the Tennessee Widow's Pension Law on July 19, 1905 for which she was given the sum of $13 per month. She stated in her application that she had one cow, a little household and kitchen furniture worth $35, and a tract of mountain land assessed to her with the title in litigation.

She was described in her application by two witnesses as being "a woman of good moral character, had not remarried, and had no means of support." She spent her final years living with her youngest daughter, Matilda, and husband, Elijah Crawford, until she passed away on Monday, June 12, 1911. Amanda was buried beside her beloved Green.

The author at Bowser Cemetery, hand on G. B. Gilbert headstone

The squirrel skin-covered Bible had a unique history, but I am not sure in whose possession it eventually ended up. From old family histories, it appears that the Bible originally belonged to Harvey Greenville Gilbert, Green Berry's father. Harvey apparently gave it to his first son, John H., who then gave it to his brother, Green Berry, before heading off to the Civil War. We know that John was killed in December 1864, shortly before the end of the war. Upon Green Berry's death, it passed to his first son, John James. John James must have given it to his last child, Clay Carson, who then gave it to his nephew, Reverend John Warren Gilbert, when he was pastor of the McPheeters Bend Missionary Baptist Church in Church Hill, Tennessee, from June 1956 to July 1961.

The trail gets cold at that point, so if anyone in the family who is reading this and has further information about this Bible, please contact me at dgilbert0776@gmail.com. I would love to find its whereabouts if, in fact, it still exists.

Author's Note

Following Green Berry Gilbert were these succeeding generations in the author's line:

William Baxter Gilbert, Sr., December 14, 1869–June 25, 1936
    (Moved to Fremont County, Iowa, circa 1903)
William Baxter Gilbert, Jr., January 10, 1905–December 31, 1965
Harold Gene Gilbert, February 24, 1925–August 5, 2011
The author, Dale E. Gilbert
(Son) Douglas D. Gilbert, (Daughter) Stacy A. (Gilbert) Dam
(Grandchildren) Hazel E. Gilbert, William D. Gilbert, Porter C. Dam, Cadence L. Dam

Acknowledgments

This is a work of historical fiction wherein I have attempted to weave together historical fact and imaginative fiction, depicting scenes of life from a previous time.

The life and times of Green Berry Gilbert and his wife, Amanda, and of the men and women in America during the 19th century is based on historical research. From this research, I have tried to recreate the emotional, physical, and spiritual setting of my family at that time.

Because of the day-to-day struggles and the monumental conflict of their lifetimes, the Civil War, I chose characters that would help draw a picture of Green Berry's life. These characters are both historical and fictional. Green Berry's older brother, John, truly was a casualty of the Civil War approximately five months before the South surrendered. Military records and written family history bear out many of the details of his service. The military leaders mentioned are also historical.

The foundation for this book was gleaned from a family history compiled by descendants of the Gilbert Family. The book is identified as follows:

The Gilberts: Roots in Virginia
by Descendants

It is a first edition with a first printing in May 1983. I have copy number 13 of 150 copies.

I relied heavily on this book to get a feel for where we came from and the various lineages that make up our family. The book is quite extensive and covers many generations. I did further research by reviewing various US Census Reports, along with military records, recording of land deeds, birth, death, and marriage licenses, etc.

I also researched the history of Company A, Twelfth Battalion, Tennessee Cavalry, Army of Tennessee to learn the whereabouts of both John and Green Berry during their service in the Civil War, which takes up a good portion of the book. The movements of the Twelfth Battalion and the battles they were involved in are as historically real as I can possibly make them. A map was included to give the reader some understanding as to the area they were in. There may be some omissions regarding certain skirmishes during this time, but I believe the narrative of the major battles is fairly accurate.

Just to clarify several points in the book, first, the author took some liberties in writing about the dedication of the new church and school on September 29, 1877. There is no evidence to support this public dedication. However, the actual land conveyance is word for word from the original, handwritten document. Second, Green Berry's first sermon in the new church on January 13, 1878, and his final sermon on August 25, 1901, are products of the author's pen. We can be sure that he preached in this very church during this time span although there are no written records to my knowledge of his sermons. However, wouldn't it have been wonderful to have heard him! The author merely tried to give several examples of what his sermons could have been like as he preached to the Dunkard Brethren.

Unless otherwise noted, all Bible scripture in this book is taken from the King James Version. Finally, all the letters exchanged between Green Berry and Amanda during the war are products of my imagination including his final love letter to her as he was dying. I wanted to portray the love between them in as many ways as I could. It was great fun to look at the iconic photo of them and imagine their thoughts and feelings as they were living through these times.

If other family members have information that will add to the clarity of this book, I welcome the input. I am no historian and simply wanted to write a story about my real family during real times in history. If my portrayal of certain historical events is somewhat lacking, I apologize to all historians and history buffs. I consider myself an above-average history buff, and any errors or omissions are entirely unintentional.

Dale E. Gilbert
Grand Island, Nebraska
March 31, 2021

About the Author

Born and raised in Hamburg, Iowa, Dale's roots go back to Southwest Virginia and eastern Tennessee.

Dale has been an avid reader all his life and has wanted to write a book for decades. Through researching his family history, he discovered an iconic great-great-grandfather.

He has a great love for American history and, in 2018, completed a sixteen-year quest to visit all the presidential libraries.

Dale holds degrees of BS and MBA as well as a graduate degree in banking.

He is a retired chief financial officer whose career spanned retailing, telecommunications, and banking.